D0379374

Lean Out

Lean Out

Dawn Foster

Foreword by Nina Power

Published by Repeater Books
An imprint of Watkins Media Ltd
19-21 Cecil Court
London
WC2N 4EZ
UK

www.repeaterbooks.com
A Repeater Books paperback original 2016
1

Distributed in the United States by Random House, Inc., New York.

Copyright © Dawn Foster 2015

Dawn Foster asserts the moral right to be identified as the author of this work.

Cover design: Johnny Bull
Typography and typesetting: Jan Middendorp
Typefaces: Chaparral Pro and Brandon Text
Printed and bound in Finland

ISBN: 978-1-910924-02-0
Ebook ISBN: 978-1-910924-03-7

All rights reserved. No part of this publication may be reproduced, stored in a retrieval system, or transmitted, in any form or by any means, electronic, mechanical, photocopying, recording or otherwise, without the prior permission of the publishers.

This book is sold subject to the condition that it shall not, by way of trade or otherwise, be lent, re-sold, hired out or otherwise circulated without the publisher's prior consent in any form of binding or cover other than that in which it is published and without a similar condition including this condition being imposed on the subsequent purchaser.

CONTENTS

To Kirsty Connell-Skinner

FOREWORD

Feminism, as Dawn Foster nimbly argues in *Lean Out*, suffers horribly from multiple claims made in its name. Criticising 'individualist' feminism, 'choice' feminism, 'corporate' feminism, 'imperialist' feminism and all the other right-wing hellspawn positions that proliferate today under its banner, Foster seeks to return to what actually matters to feminism, and what mattered all along: class, economics, poverty, race, violence, workplace struggles, childcare, policy, anti-capitalism and the role of the state. And Dawn knows what she's talking about. Her accounts of working zero hours contract jobs and her critiques of the endless *Guardian*-style 'can you be a feminist and...' (own monkeys? lick the end of pens? wear odd socks? etc. etc. etc.) stem from her experiences as a working class woman and a journalist (she wins prizes for her coverage of social and housing issues). I like Dawn a lot, not least because she refuses to take any shit from anyone, be it editor, man on Twitter, right-wing pundit she's arguing with on Sky or Newsnight or her friends. She reminds me of the kind of investigative journalist that has historically been extinguished under press releases and the diminution of print media. But yet still she lives!

Dawn's book is timely. Current poster-woman for corporate feminism, billionaire Sheryl Sandberg represents what we might call 'oblivious' feminism: the kind that has to ignore global financial crises, government austerity policies and ingrained sexism in order to argue that feminism is a kind of moral or existential decision: 'If I look really perky in this boring meeting and come up with some good ideas, maybe I'll get a pat on the head and a raise in thirty-five years!' 'If I pretend that childcare provisions at my workplace are really good when in fact they're awful, perhaps the boss will notice me and give me a promotion!' When Sandberg describes an 'ambition gap' amongst women in corporate environments, she cannot possibly ask herself what might be wrong with capitalism itself such that many women have no or little interest, or ability, to bridge such a 'gap'. The gap is less the problem than the system that depends upon the gap, and no amount of over-conforming and 'playing the game' is going to get rid of it.

But Dawn's work is careful and much less grandstanding than the kind of claims I generally tend to make: she tirelessly ploughs through figures, stats and policy to back up her arguments, and inserts personal reflection at key junctures to fill out her analytic points. It's a style that exemplifies the best in contemporary writing: political without being bombastic, fact-heavy without being dry. It's also wry and sarcastic when it needs to be, because the world is a tiring and unfair place, and we cannot live in it without humour.

Nina Power, August 2015

CHAPTER 1

Leaning In

Not too long ago, hearing the word "viral", whether in a film or a doctor's surgery, would cause a certain amount of alarm. Viruses in films invariably signal a cataclysmic, dystopian scenario, a hitherto unknown incurable disease that threatens the entire existence of the human race around the globe. When a doctor, removing the blood-pressure strap from your arm, informs you that you have a viral rather than bacterial infection, you know you have to sit it out and attempt to take the edge off the symptoms, rather than being sent off with a pack of antibiotics that will cure you in a few days.

It's strange then that the term has changed so swiftly to a broadly positive term for a story, meme, or video clip that becomes wildly, uncontrollably popular online very quickly. The fascination with what "goes viral" is down to the unpredictability of the internet, and by extension the unpredictability of human beings. Advertisers and media agencies try, and usually fail, to replicate the style of videos and articles that go viral. Newspapers and websites rush to either write or respond to viral content in an attempt to siphon off some of the web traffic.

One such viral success was, perhaps counterintuitively, a short lecture on women in the workplace. *Lean In* began as a TED talk, delivered in December 2011 by Facebook's Chief Operating Officer Sheryl Sandberg under the title "Why we have too few female leaders". In the 15-minute video Sandberg argued that the main reason women aren't rising to the top, aren't getting that feted "corner office", is a lack of assertiveness, an unwilling-ness to put themselves forward.

She encouraged the audience, in the room and watching on screens globally, to "make their partner a real partner" — choose a husband who would do half the childcare and housework — and finally, she implored women "don't leave before you leave", by which, Sandberg explained, she meant she was tired of seeing women lower their career ambitions years before even trying to conceive, let alone getting pregnant, leaving them with no desirable career to return to once they had children.

This reticence amongst women to put themselves forward for promotion and negotiate salaries was responsible for the slow growth in women at the very top. These character traits may be unarguably common, but Sandberg is perennially afraid to scrutinise why this may be. Instead, these behavioural tropes in women's approaches to work, and the so-called "ambition gap", are mentioned but not explored.

The reason this lecture became popular is not too difficult to see: women's inequality in the workplace is a stubborn problem that seems unrelenting and immovable. Offering a solution, especially one that is personally achievable, is tantalising in its simplicity. Few want to run the risk of not watching a video that promises you personal success. Self-help books fly off shelves in shops because they promise a better life, whilst simultaneously feeding off the fact that most people are still unhappy with themselves, because it's difficult to feel you ever have enough. Capitalism mandates that everyone be in perpetual competition with each other. This naturally spills over into personal, as well as professional, lives.

On 21st January 2014, Sandberg became a billionaire. Articles popped up proclaiming this as a symbol of women's collective progress, as Sandberg was one of only 12 female billionaires globally not to have inherited or married into her fortune.

Feminism, popular narratives would have you believe, is an onward march towards a tangibly close emancipation — one that all women of different social and economic situations are engaged in. The "Glass Ceiling", we're told, is the barrier, and chipping away slowly at it is the firmest, surest way to the final goal of gender equality. This is the premise behind Sandberg's business manifesto, which also functions as a personal employment memoir. We're in a better position now, as a gender, than we've ever been. Sandberg uses the image of women in developing nations to invoke horror at other women's position in comparison to that of the westernised, emancipated and business-oriented woman she is addressing.

As Kate Losse, Sandberg's former colleague, pointed out, for all of her talk of "internalising the revolution" and name-dropping Betty Friedan, "Sandberg has penned not so much a new Feminine Mystique as an updated Protestant Ethic and the Spirit of Capitalism".[1] Sandberg's corporate feminism doesn't extend to calling for collective rights for women such as state maternity pay, or a stronger welfare safety net, or even encouraging women to unionise. *Lean In* sold well, and was accompanied by a whole branded media platform, including *Lean In* circles, where women are encouraged to discuss "positive" thoughts around work and how to get ahead. It wasn't so well read, however: Amazon Kindle listed it as one of the books least likely to be finished, cementing its reputation as a lifestyle brand, rather than a life solution. On the subject of the *Lean In* brand, Melissa Gira Grant observes: "This is simply the elite leading the slightly-less-elite, for the sake of Sandberg's bottom line. The 'movement' Sandberg seeks to lead with *Lean In* resembles a social movement only so far as it supports the growth of her brand as leader."[2]

Corporate feminism is easy to sell—who could baulk at the idea of getting more women into fields where there are few? And the ideals on which it trades—personal development, confidence, nurturing family—are politically helpful in focusing on individual success stories, rather than structural inequality and looking outwith the organisations that women are struggling to gain promotions within. Corporate feminism tells us that aspiration and success is within everyone's reach if they endeavour to try hard enough, a message which has the unuttered flipside that failure is also down to the individual not wanting it enough. "Never mind that your boss is sexist, or maternity leave in America punishingly short", says Gaby Hinsliff in *The Observer*, "Sandberg says you just need to 'raise your hand' more and you'll rise".[3]

One reason why corporate feminism is so palatable where previous incarnations have been antagonistic to the establishment and status quo, is that it is completely non-confrontational. As Gira Grant argues:

> Anyone who knows anything about the tech biz knows that this is a (social) media side show, and that feminism will never be one of the 'disruptive' values of Silicon Valley so long as Silicon Valley is principally a machine for producing wealth for the few. To the extent that someone who so benefits from that business culture espouses feminism, it will be ruthlessly friendly to the corporate environment in which it is exercised. [4]

Lean In points all blame inward, and ignores structural inequality—the biggest reason women are still lagging in the workplace is "the ambition gap", we're told. Sandberg opines: "And while the ambition gap is most pronounced at the highest levels, the underlying dynamic is evident at every stage of the career ladder." What causes this ambition gap? Why does it increase as women get further in their career? There's no attempt at analysis, or acknowledgment that ambition is a moot point when inequality remains so entrenched in modern society. A woman working as a receptionist in a small business can aspire to be a chief executive of a high-street bank all she wants, but without a stellar education and the attendant social connections high-ranking universities furnish alumni with, she may as well aspire to be a unicorn for all the good it will do.

Ambition without realism is megalomania: the majority of people have a fairly accurate idea of where their professional life could take them. While young children often aspire to be footballers, astronauts, princesses, most people from their mid-teens onwards have an awareness of their limits. I will never be the head of an investment bank, or a train driver, but jobs in writing and research aren't remotely unlikely. Someone who dropped out of school before their GCSEs will be aware that their chances of becoming a surgeon are vastly diminished, but being a manager within a construction company might be possible with intense effort.

Ambition is tempered not just by individual whim, but by the codes and messages people pick up on throughout their lives, fractured by gender, class, race, sexuality and levels of disability. Telling women to ignore their inner barometer of their own likely success is hardly a solution. A woman may be as ambitious as she wants, but the people hiring and firing have their own preconceptions, in a society that maintains that women are less decisive, logical and driven. If a woman's ambitions exceed the ambition her superiors feel is appropriate, wanting can do barely anything—you're still stuck on the pay grade your managers have attributed to you.

Shaky Ground

When women do reach the top spot, their tenure is rarely as secure as their male counterparts. Two high-profile departures in a week in 2014, *The New York Times'* executive editor Jill Abramson and *Le Monde*'s Natalie Nougayrède, coincided with a report from researchers at global management consultant Strategy& that showed female Chief Executives are forced out of top jobs sooner than male counterparts.[5] Strategy&'s report suggested female CEOs tended to be outsiders, hired in, rather than climbing to the top within the ranks of an organisation, so faced double hostility: both sexism from colleagues and the perception that others who had worked for years within the organisation had been unfairly been passed over.

There was also the observation that women tended to be appointed to failing organisations, and then sacked for the very failings of the business: whether women were more likely to take on the challenge, or businesses were less likely to assign male candidates to sinking ships remains unclear. But women's sackings remain pored over more publicly and are afforded far shorter shrift.

When Carole Bartz was sacked from Yahoo in 2011 shortly after taking on the failing company, she told *Fortune* magazine: "These people fucked me over. The board was so spooked by being cast as the worst board in the country. Now they're trying to show that they're not the doofuses that they are." When the interviewer mentioned her age—63—and asked her what she was planning to do next, she responded "Fuck you—yeah".[6] The *Guardian* described it as "a foul-mouthed tirade", and it's difficult not to feel that if a male CEO had indulged in the same language it would be described merely as an "outburst" and marked them out as a colourful character in a back-slapping, macho tech environment.

Leaning Back

Fascinatingly, Sandberg attributes this purported stasis in the number of women in top jobs to an acculturated belief by women that they won't get to the board room, a "leaning back"—essentially, the only thing holding women back from achieving their "best potential" in the workplace is their own self-defeatism. One staggering omission in a book that is so focused on business, boardrooms, and capitalism looms over *Lean In* like a shadow and could easily explain why there aren't more women in the higher echelons of FTSE and Fortune companies, since it certainly accounts for the rise in working-class women's pay squeezes: the global financial crisis.

Research by Emily Thomson and Susanne Ross at Glasgow Caledonian University shows that although women's workforce participation is now at its highest rate in Britain since records began, post-crash, women's jobs are increasingly casual, precarious and low-paid:

> Total employment is now higher than pre-recession levels, with female employment currently at the highest since comparable records began. Since economic recovery took hold in 2010, total employment has increased by 2.1 million; men increased their employment by 1.2 million compared to 910,000 for women. The male employment rate therefore rose slightly faster than the female employment rate, increasing by 3.5% compared to 3.1% for women.[7]

When recovery happens, it works best for men, and when recession happens, it hits women harder.

On 20th February 2014, right-leaning tabloids and broadsheets boomed with the news that employment was up, and more women were in work than at any point in history. *The Times* put this down to "cuts to benefits and the rising pension age", as though a few snatched pounds from a subsistence state handouts at either end of their life was forcing women away from their life of leisure and into the workforce. On the front page of the *Telegraph*, John Philpott, director of the consultancy firm Jobs Economist, said "One of the interesting things about the female employment story has been that austerity was expected to hit them hardest, as two in three public sector workers are women. As it is, women either were hit disproportionately lightly or they have found it easier to move into the private sector."

This analysis only works if the only women you consider are women in work. And in many ways, political discourse does only consider those in-work people — the deadening mantra of "hard-working families" has become so hackneyed a phrase it's become impossible to take any politician uttering it in the

House of Commons seriously. Yet, without fail, it springs forth from someone's lips if you have the misfortune of watching *Prime Minister's Questions* on any given Wednesday.

Despite the improving jobs picture, the gender pay-gap in the United Kingdom widened in 2013 for the first time since 2008, and for only the second time since the 1970s. Analysis of ONS figures by the TUC suggested that the gap was 15.7% on average in December, or the equivalent of £5,000 a year for an average woman. Drill down even further, and the prospects look grimmer if you're older: the average woman in her fifties can expect to earn £11.99 an hour—18% less than the £14.69 a man of the same age would currently earn.

Small Scope

When offering up advice on how women can achieve the ideal work-life balance, tellingly, Sandberg never envisages an image of a woman as anything other than a worker, or a wife and mother. The alpha successful women in *Lean In* are always bouncing between boardrooms and babies, and the Lean Backs are daydreaming about promotions, or longing for the perfect husband and fretting over imagined biological clocks. There is no room, in the corporate feminist world, for a civil life, a political life, an emotional life outside of the nuclear family unit, or even downtime. All time is accounted for, and if a woman is not putting in her full attention at work, the only possible explanation is that she is dropping out to procreate, rather than that—heaven forbid—she might not like her job, or may have outside pursuits that sustain her interest more fully.

Lean In relies heavily on chummy anecdotes, but speaks with complete conviction of how Sandberg's experience in a very niche sector can embolden women to achieve professional success. "Without fear", Sandberg says, "women can pursue professional success and personal fulfilment." Not quite—structural inequalities and discriminations prevent professional success and personal fulfilment. The woman working a minimum-wage cleaning job in a Silicon Valley office is less likely to find Sandberg's conversational pay negotiation skills remotely helpful: there's still a stark divide between "a career" and "a job".

Such levelling happened in Birmingham City Council in England for years — jobs traditionally filled with employees from only one gender (e.g. for women: dinner ladies, care workers and cleaners; and for men: refuse operatives and security guards) received similar pay. But "male" jobs covertly received a host of benefits — overtime, antisocial hour upticks and bonuses — which meant in essence they were paid far more than women for jobs on the same skill level. When they discovered this and began to pursue a discrimination claim for equal pay, their union — the GMB — encouraged the women to drop the claim, or risk men having their pay lowered to match the women's. Essentially, the women were asked to forget pursuing equal pay, purely so as not to achieve equal pay at the detriment of men's finances. Rightly, they ignored the GMB's advice, and in 2014 after a long legal battle, were awarded back pay so high, Birmingham council were forced to sell their National Exhibition Centre to settle the costs.

The Outliers
The conversation around feminism seems to have stalled, and focuses on individual "aces" within feminism rather than the power of collective agitation. As Judith Shulevitz explains in an article in *The New Republic*:

> We're still talking about mentors, glass ceilings, and the impossibility or desirability of having it all. What we are not talking about in nearly enough detail, or agitating for with enough passion, are the government policies, such as mandatory paid maternity leave, that would truly equalize opportunity. We are still thinking individually, not collectively.[8]

Sandberg has worked in government and in large Silicon Valley organisations, but neatly tiptoes around governmental and corporate responsibilities to women, and how the US's lack of paid maternity leave directly discriminates against working women. Whereas the UK and many other industrialised countries have a minimum period of paid maternity leave (and some paid paternity leave), the US offers only three months of unpaid maternity leave. Even if the government refused to act, corporations could move to offer genuine working rights. But of course, profit margins are more important than women's opportunities in the workplace.

Instead, the focus in Sandberg's book, and in so many articles on contemporary feminism, is on the individual, especially the individual in the nuclear family unit. This seems almost quaint in its outlook, considering increasing numbers of women are not having children at all, and divorce rates are higher than they've ever been. Until, that is, you look at the kinds of women who actually make up the upper echelons of industry. For men, marriage symbolises stability—the candidate who is married with existing children is a safer punt than the one who might spend his nights prowling around bars. For women, being young signals your fertility and implies that you may leave and have children. The fact that not everyone is enamoured with the idea of pregnancy and childrearing is unthinkable when considering women.

The importance of "aspiration" over equality both focuses on individual success, and in turn attributes failure to individuals, rather than a system designed to promote a few, transferring wealth to the "aspirational" at the expense of many, many others. Rather than admit that life chances, and the lack thereof, stifle ambition and outright block financial and professional achievements for poorer citizens, a society that promotes "aspiration" must rely on outliers. Interviews with the newly rich from humble and disadvantaged beginnings reveal a tendency not to rail against the injustices systemic inequality perpetuates, but instead to turn inward, focussing on individual achievement as proof that these barriers do not exist for those who pull themselves up by their bootstraps.

Personally, this isn't surprising: jumping class barriers often leads to loneliness, both in the distance felt from friends and family who remain in the now alien situation you were born into, and in the social sphere you now find yourself in – unable to read codes and markers, and internalising the scorn cast your way if you appear boorish at a black-tie drinks do, pick up the wrong fork when served dinner, or find yourself dressed inappropriately at an event. Social mobility can be an isolating experience, and the attendant shame of your background encourages you to denigrate it, castigating those who haven't succeeded in breaking the mould and finding themselves in a high-paying job, earning far more than their young peers and family ever imagined was possible.

But without outliers, it is difficult for a cult of aspiration to justify itself. Ideologies need stories, individuals to hold up as exemplary figures, lives that are proof of their mantra. Sheryl Sandberg provides that perfectly for corporate feminism, as Nicole Ascherhoff notes:

> Like many prophets before her, Sandberg makes her case by telling the story of her own path to success. Sandberg worked her way up to the top from middle class beginnings: her father was an ophthalmologist, her mother was a French teacher turned stay-at-home mom. She graduated from Harvard, twice, and has worked in high-powered jobs at the US Treasury, and now Google. Industry types consider her a "rock star in business, politics, and popular culture with unprecedented influence and reach".[9]

As an example of feminine success, purporting to share her secrets, Sandberg acts as a face for business – a talisman proving that capitalism can welcome women if they *lean in* and change their self-destructive behaviours. It is individual failures, not a structure designed to keep businesses homogenous, that keeps the gender pay-gap in place and forces an earnings cut on women who have the audacity to have children.

Corporate feminism seeks to exhibit extremely rich women, not as symbols of our increasingly unequal society and distribution of wealth, but as saviours of womanhood: because they have succeeded, now you can too. Their wealth is a step forward for women because wealth trickles down, and so too does aspiration. It's difficult to accept that your position in life is down to luck, privilege and coincidence far more than sheer talent. So people lap up individual success stories, and trawl over details of CEOs' daily routines, looking for the secret habits that cause these people to be so successful.

As comforting as the idea of "trickledown feminism" might be, it's never borne out in reality—the four most powerful jobs in Norway are held by women,[10] yet politicians are considering allowing doctors to refuse to perform abortions. The slowly shrinking gender disparity of MPs is constantly held up as a marker of progress, yet at the same time, Rachel Reeves promises to be "tougher" than the Tories when it comes to savaging the welfare state,[11] and Theresa May, the UK home secretary, has overseen conditions in the Yarl's Wood women's immigration detention centre worsen under her watch.

The problem with corporate feminism's obsession with individual stories of success, and "having it all",[12] is that many women don't have much at all. Women have been disproportionately affected by austerity,[13] with single mothers and pensioners particularly affected. A few more women may be MPs or CEOs, but three times as many young women are locked into low-paid jobs than were 20 years ago.[14] The fall in real-term wages affects women more, since women were earning less in the first place.[15] Asking women to "lean in" is far easier than demanding that we fundamentally change the way businesses operate, who they operate for, and how we reward and approach work.

Corporate feminism tells a story that is convenient to capitalism. If personal aspiration is the key to success for women, and emancipation is to be won on an individual basis for you and your hardworking family, then solidarity and the prospect of structural and legal change becomes a pointless distraction. Focusing on individual success stories, rather than structural inequality, is politically helpful to the right-wing squeeze on living standards across Europe and the United States. If you're languishing at the bottom of the corporate ladder rather than hammering on the glass ceiling, blame yourself, not the power structures that conspire to shrink your life chances. Anyone could be Sheryl Sandberg, Melissa Mayer, or a female Bill Gates if they want it enough. That the richest people in the world are predominantly white, male, and stale is pure coincidence.

CHAPTER 2

Lehman Sisters

"Women's work and women's labour are buried deeply in the heart of the capitalist social economic structure." — DAVID STAPLES, *No Place Like Home*

A quip, originating with Christine Lagarde but repeated by Harriet Harman, is that Lehman Brothers would never have collapsed and precipitated the financial crisis if it were "Lehman Sisters". The subtext—that women are by their nature more reserved, less risk-taking, more responsible—props up the idea that the problem wasn't the economic system, but purely the individuals pulling the levers responsible for plunging most of the globe into a long-reaching recession.

The system then, is only broken until the boards are shuffled and shaken up a little. A few women in the boardroom will shake up the whole culture of the company—corporate social responsibility will become not a begrudging sop to not getting sued, but a seamless and easy part of company life. Perhaps the only reason the financial crash even happened wasn't because of rapacious capitalism and intensive corporate lobbying of governments in favour of laissez-faire or non-existent market regulation, but simply because there were more people called John in the company than women in total.

Post-crash, the focus on gender balance at the top of multinationals has intensified, while the political will amongst the establishment to control the mechanisms that enabled the financial crash has waned. Speaking on Glencore Xstrata's failure to appoint a female director to the board, then UK Business Secretary Vince Cable said in May 2014: "The vast majority of Britain's top companies have got the message that a diverse top management team is good for business—it is simply not credible that one company cannot find any suitable women." It might be good for business, either if you buy the argument that women intrinsically change the way businesses run, or accept that a diverse board makes a business seem less Machiavellian. But is it good for women?

Diversity here, rather than being a sign that indirect or direct discrimination hasn't taken place in the recruitment and appointment procedures, is framed as "good for business". Former banker and government minister, and current man, Lord Davies, was charged with producing a report for the Department for Business Innovation and Skills on the lack of representation of women in FTSE 100 boardrooms in 2011. In a section headed "More women on boards—why does it matter?" he states:

> The issues debated here are as much about improving business performance as about promoting equal opportunities for women. There is a strong business case for balanced boards. Inclusive and diverse boards are more likely to be effective boards, better able to understand their customers and stakeholders and to benefit from fresh perspectives, new ideas, vigorous challenge and broad experience. This in turn leads to better decision making.[16]

The argument that diversity makes any organisation better by widening the pool of talent is accepted in all but the most elitist and backwards-looking organisations and institutions. The reason why lack of diversity is criticised is because it is a symptom of social exclusion of women, black candidates, and candidates with disability. To argue that you have an all-white, all-male board is to argue that the men are just better, and that the groups not represented in the higher echelons of business and commerce simply aren't capable or smart enough. Of course, people still do argue this, claiming it's a coincidence that the candidates for each individual job or promotion happened to mirror the demographic already holding forth in the corner offices. But too many coincidences raise suspicion. If every time you ask somebody to watch your pet dog it escapes, you might be inclined to think this happens less by chance than negligence.

Large conglomerates are waking up to the idea that the lack of women at higher levels delivers them an image problem that is difficult to shake. The argument is that the world is merito-cratic and well-paid jobs, awards, financial rewards gravitate to those who deserve them and work hard for the lavish spoils of their labour. But when your offices are full of men — and almost entirely white, straight men — the question "So are women and black people simply not good enough?" becomes an awkward one, with no answer that affords the company a veneer of respectability.

But the clamour for a "Lehman Sisters" handily circum-vents the discussion on whether our financial institutions and models, which remain largely unchanged post-crash, are fit for purpose, whoever is on the board. Some of the culture, macho and drug-fuelled, around the time of the crash, especially in high-frequency trading, was down to the male-dominated sector. But a lot of women were still in high-ranking positions in US banks and government, and still failed to regulate risky and illegal behaviour, not because of their gender, but because of the accepted narrative that capitalism flourishes when it is unrestrained. The free market is all. There are not simply two cultures in each society: male and female. Class, race, education and social status, as well as gender, all combine to build individ-uals and have competing interests.

When I was working for a brief period for a magazine in Canary Wharf, the slightly out-of-town financial hub in east London, acting as an amateur anthropologist in bars, shops, and cafes was fascinating. The area was home to several large investment banks, accounting firms, and other multinationals, and incorporated two large underground shopping centres, filled with shops selling luxury jewellery, platinum watches, high-end clothes, and cosmetics. The pavements and gardens were spotless: arriving at the break of dawn one morning to meet a deadline, I saw a middle-aged man using a vacuum-cleaner on a stretch of grass. A Norwegian friend, shocked at the gleaming skyscrapers and scrubbed streets, declared that it was "like Dubai landed in a normal city".

In bars and cafes, the women were just as belligerent and snobbish to the baristas and waiting staff as the men. Waiting to board the Underground, the elbow sending you glancing away from an available seat while you were on crutches was just as likely to belong to a besuited person of either gender. Men were slightly more numerous, but the behaviour concomitant with the area was cross-gender: less an air, more a stench, of entitlement and a self-satisfied arrogance hung about the place. The employment of some women didn't act like an air freshener, subtly sweetening the culture. Establishments don't tend to welcome outsiders if they aren't willing to play by the rules, and fit into existing structures.

A 2013 survey commissioned by the 30% Club, a group of companies pushing for more women on boards, found that women still weren't filling prestigious roles in companies, including boardroom roles.[17] Interviewing over 500 women and men in 13 blue-chip companies, researchers found that male executives were more likely to be seen as rational and decisive. By contrast, women were seen as well-organised and ethical, which in turn had a detrimental effect on their chances of promotion. Being methodical and value-driven are desirable traits in middle-ranking roles in companies, but recruiters still seek "decision-makers" for managerial roles, and subconsciously associate that trait with men. "Women are seen as being very values-led and very good about being able to direct people to 'do the right thing'," Rachel Short, director of YSC business psychologists, told *The Guardian* newspaper. "Men were seen as being very good at rational and analytical decision making."

Stereotypes about women being less rational and more emotional than men are partly to blame when it comes to the recruitment process. The survey, as with any discussion on boardrooms and getting "women on top", attracted a lot of attention and debate—far more than reports on women being hit harder by poverty or finding it harder to bring discriminatory employers to industrial tribunals ever do. For decades, the measure of success for the feminist movement in some quarters has simply been how many women are present at the very top, regardless of what happens to the bulk of women at the very bottom of society.

Because it is unchallenging, corporate feminism is easy to sell, as issues go. As a branding exercise it works—personal stories about women who have climbed the corporate ladder and smashed the glass ceiling play well and are treated as instruction manuals, rather than, by virtue of their rarity, a condemnation of an unequitable society. Mary T Barra, the first female head of General Motors, "completed a remarkable personal odyssey" in becoming the company chief, *The New York Times* reported. Her "remarkable personal odyssey" seems to have comprised of being a woman, whilst doing her job.

Few women will sit in boardrooms in their lifetime, and adding a few "golden skirts"[18] in places of high responsibility doesn't translate straight to a hastening improvement in women's rights and quality of life. Research has shown that most women on Norwegian boards are in non-executive positions.[19] It's far easier to discuss why so few women are in boardrooms than it is to discuss why so many women claim housing benefit. A woman elbowing her way into the boardroom seems winnable, and doing so is often treated as a tangible and measurable win for feminism.

But feminism isn't a linear march, progressing slowly and inevitably. Listing rights won is a common way to show how far women's emancipation has come. But reproductive rights, economic empowerment, and even suffrage rights are all under threat. In the 2015 budget, the Conservative Chancellor George Osborne announced a "two child policy", stopping child benefit at two children. If you have three, you won't receive the small benefit allowance for the third. This cut will in effect take up to £2,780 per child per year from working families in receipt of tax credits.

Except in two cases—if you have twins on your second pregnancy, or if you have been raped and the pregnancy has resulted from that rape. The documents state that "The Department for Work and Pensions and HMRC will develop protections for women who have a third child as a result of rape, or other exceptional circumstances." In effect, this means a rape test—requiring women to prove they have been raped before they are allowed to receive child benefit for their baby. Nothing has been said as to what evidence may be required, but with under-reporting of rape running at 80–90% and convicted rapes still alarmingly low, it's difficult to know exactly what women can be expected to do, especially after enduring a traumatic crime.

In effect, the government is signalling that poor women are to blame for their own poverty, and children are by-and-large a luxury for the rich to participate in. As Nancy Fraser argues, poor women are particularly vulnerable to exploitation: "Needy women with no other way to feed themselves and their children, for example, are liable to exploitation—by abusive husbands, by sweatshops foremen, by pimps. In guaranteeing relief of poverty, then, welfare provision should also aim to mitigate exploitable dependency."[20] Despite the fact that more than half of working families are in poverty, the Victorian idea that the poor breed like rabbits when they should be sterilised seems to be taking hold again. At the same time, the Child Support Agency has slowly been phased out, leaving mothers with little hope of gaining maintenance payments from absent fathers.

For women at the bottom, the gender of whoever is pulling the strings at the top makes little difference if the political administration is still firmly in favour of the powerful, who by pure coincidence happen to be rich, male professionals.

CHAPTER 3

Having It All

"Can women have it all?" asked (what seemed like) every third commentator in the West for a period after the turn of the millennium. "Super Mums" appeared in glossy magazine features declaring that having seven children, a magazine catalogue-esque husband, a minimalist yet chic house, *and* a directorship or twelve was effortless, aside from a few light strategical negotiations. Super Mums are invariably wealthier than the readers of weekend supplements, and when asked about how they manage, they never respond: "I hired a number of women to work for low wages, cleaning and running my household, carrying out life admin, organising my diary, and raising my children." Mothers on minimum wage who manage to keep a job, raise children, and run households are never deemed Super Mums, only Irresponsible Mums for having the audacity to have children in the first place.

It is having-it-all that Sandberg is particularly concerned with in parts of *Lean In*. The "baby trap" women fall into in careers is classified by Sandberg as a trap of individual women's own making. Sandberg herself admits to being back on work email from her hospital room the day after the birth of her first son, and organising meetings in her home during the paltry three months of maternity leave Google offered her.[21]

"If society truly valued the work of caring for children, companies and institutions would find ways to reduce these steep penalties and help parents combine career responsibilities",[22] Sandberg says, before complaining that too many women, when realising going back to work doesn't cover the childcare costs, leave. Rather than ask why work doesn't pay, and why having children should be deemed a luxury lifestyle choice, as opposed to an economic necessity in any country that wants to grow. America gets it wrong, and then wonders why women drop out of the workplace. Sandberg's solution: to continue working for a loss until you eventually get promoted, all the while missing your children growing up. This will only work for some women, and is unlikely to work at all for the lowest-paid women, who are given hourly rates set by head offices rather than being able to negotiate a salary and manoeuvre into their own career path with plenty of professional development and flexibility. Furthermore, Sandberg doesn't suggest what the "ways to reduce these steep penalties and help parents combine career responsibilities" might be. The problem is that if you are not at work, you are not generating profit — a thought unpalatable to corporations.

The inconvenient fact is, women have children, and will continue to have children. People in many countries are having fewer children (often due to recession and economic hardship) or having them later, but populations as a whole haven't stopped procreating. And while women have children, the annoying question of how to handle that continues to rear its ugly head. In workplaces, there is still a huge level of resentment toward women who dare to get pregnant, and a suspicion that successful women have "gamed the system" by planning pregnancies shortly after promotions in order to maximise their maternity pay, or to cheat a male colleague out of a job, while plotting to have the best of both worlds, and leave the job in order to sit at home playing with a baby for several months.

The idea that women get it easy with maternity leave is an alien concept to anyone who has had a baby: after nine months of exhaustion, a further year or more of sleeplessness and constantly attending to a small and helpless creature who finds it impossible to communicate initially is far more gruelling than the grind of office life. At least you can sleep through the night after a week of spreadsheets. But the problems persist after maternity leave: women return, feeling out of the loop as several months of office life has passed without them, new colleagues hired, routines and processes changed, and many women struggle to find their footing again.

Sandberg warns against women psychologically and emotionally checking out of jobs before they leave for maternity (and the US's three-month leave is far shorter than the six-to-twelve months standard paid leave in the UK), but doesn't exam the external forces that might contribute to that. Subconscious bullying of women who become pregnant, subtle exclusion from meetings and email chains, or the fact that the company's pay is so low, and flexible working policies so threadbare, that women realise they can't afford to come back, mean that the atmosphere will only further sour.

While childcare eats into greater and greater portions of income, women are less likely to return to work and apply for promotions, or in the case of low-paid women, be able to work at all. Actual recognition by governments of the importance of women being able to work, and the provision of childcare as a state service, are solutions far more likely to yield results than chiding women for not working at a loss, or for daring to think about both their children and their career prospects. It's this argument that has garnered some Scandinavian countries a feminist fan club.

On paper, and certainly when compared to Britain and America, Scandinavia seems for all the world to be a feminist utopia. Consistently dominating global gender-equality rankings, with Denmark 8th, Sweden 4th and Norway 3rd, it makes you long to emulate their success in Britain (which ranks at a paltry 18th).[23] On paper, Scandinavian countries perform well for women, having instituted many policies that feminists in the UK have spent decades lobbying for: the aforementioned boardroom quotas; extended, shared parental leave; and state-funded childcare.

As a result, in Sweden for example, women earn 94% of what men do, on average. Forty-six percent of their MPs, and 13 out of 24 ministers, are women.[24] Economic participation is high, as women tend to return to work after having children. Norway elected their second female prime minister, Erna Solberg, in 2013. With Siv Jensen as finance minister, Gerd Kristiansen as head of the Norwegian equivalent of the TUC, and Kristin Skogen Lund leading the Confederation of Norwegian Enterprise, the four most powerful jobs in Norway are all held by women.[25]

But drilling down into the stats, and speaking to women about their day-to-day experiences, reveals some discontent behind the headline figures. While pay is on average far more equal than we've come to expect in Europe, certain sectors still lag behind. Women still struggle to attain professorships in Scandinavian universities, according to research conducted by Queen Mary University in London[26], pointing out that "women are still judged according to their potential or actual reproductive capacity", and informal recruitment practices often compound this problem. In Sweden, 64% of managers in the public sector, where they've been legally required to consider gender equality as integral to strategy, are women. In sharp contrast, a mere 4% of managing directors and board chairs in the private sector are women.[27] Norway's boardroom gender quotas have also had mixed effects: advocates argued that getting women onto boards would have a "ripple effect", promoting gender equality from the top down.[28] This has yet to be borne out.

Nowhere are women's rights more at risk than in Scandinavia's attitude towards sexual violence. Amnesty criticised low conviction rates across the region in a damning report in 2010: in Denmark, 60% of reported rapes never make it to trial, while in Norway, only 16% of cases make it to court, with 13% of those that do ending in conviction.[29] Two high-profile cases involving young, vulnerable women sparked protests in Sweden: one gang-rape, and one case in which a girl reported being raped by her foster father[30], neither of which ended in a conviction.

Much of this is down to legislative anomalies failing to protect the sexual autonomy of victims: in Sweden and Norway laws dictate that rape only occurs when accompanied by threats of physical violence. Issues around consent abound – Swedish law professor Madeleine Leijonhufvud called for laws to include stipulations that consent be given prior to sex, after a judge remarked of a 15-year-old victim in a gang-rape case that despite the act happening against her express protestations, as she was not unconscious, it was not rape.[31] Amnesty were particularly concerned by the rate of gang-rapes in Scandinavia – 29% of all reported cases, and 18% in Sweden.

The Scandinavian gender problem shows two things. Firstly, legislation can change only so much: cultural attitudes must change alongside legislation. For many young Scandinavians, equality is a given, feminism isn't a dirty word, and they're proud of their welfare state. The problem, as ever, remains in who holds power: the judiciary is still white and male, and has the power to rule using older legislation. Stories of judges making heinous remarks about young rape victims are common currency in England, but we only hear of those who are careless enough to make their prejudices known, rather than the discretely racist and sexist judges muddling along, ruining lives.

On boards too, companies claimed not enough women had the experience required (begging the question why those companies weren't recruiting enough), so boards continued recruiting only the minimum number of women, kindly allowing yet more men experience of business, enabling them to serve on many more boards in their lifetime. The public-sector and private-sector divide in gender shows just how staunch the resistance of business can be to gender parity in companies. In turn, the fact that much childcare has been formalised (rather than children being left with grandparents) has widened the gender gulf, with women vastly outnumbering men in the caring professions, and men flocking to the financial industries.

Secondly, gender equality is always in danger of being rescinded: both Norway and Sweden elected right-wing coalition governments, with traditional views on women and families. It's easy to become complacent and assume battles won for women and enshrined in legislation are battles done with, but there is always likely to be a section of the population who would happily see those rights taken back if there was an opportunity to benefit from that move.

The experience of women in Norway, Denmark, and Sweden shows there's much to be hopeful for if gender-equality legislation can be passed around the world, and in many ways, Scandinavia's as close to a feminist utopia as many of us are likely to see in our lifetime. But it also warns against complacency: women's lot is improving but precarious. The move towards a more equal society has been long fought, and much depends on economic stability: Scandinavia is rich in resources, and was spared the global recession—and as the financial crisis taught us, when austerity bites, it's women who suffer most. But quotas alone are not enough to secure gender equality, and the relative freedom the private sector is afforded shows how much is at risk when rights are removed or not bolstered. Scandinavia didn't tell citizens to lean in, it pushed back against structural sexism through imposed legislation.

CHAPTER 4

Hiring and Firing

"Now it's autumn, soon winter will come over us with snow, and I will work, I will work." — ANTON CHEKHOV, *Three Sisters*

More women in the seat of power means more women flocking in behind them, surely? If the problem is men hiring people who look and sound like them, can't women just hold the door open behind them after a surprise hiring?

Not necessarily. A recent study by the University of Colorado found that when recruited into top positions in business, women and ethnic minorities hired far less diversely than their white male counterparts, fearing that hiring candidates who looked like them, or strayed from the white male norm in these institutions, would earn them accusations of tokenism. "Women and non-white executives who push for women and non-whites to be hired and promoted suffer when it comes to their own performance reviews. A woman who shepherds women up the ranks, for example, is perceived as less warm, while a non-white who promotes diversity is perceived as less competent. Both end up being rated less highly by their bosses."[32] Daring to hire from outside the traditional pool whilst non-traditional yourself, merely ensures the prejudicial stereotypes applied to your race or gender come back to haunt you.

The double bind meant that institutions where hiring was led by white men became more diverse, then quickly stalled. The idea that once women are through the door, they'll hire more women, and in turn more women will see them in a position of power and apply themselves, neatly sidesteps the external structures that are stopping most women from reaching the top in business.

At the same time, employment rights in the UK have taken a battering, and women are bearing the brunt. The number of people on short-term contracts, mostly part-time, has soared in the past five years. Rather than focusing on getting one or two women through the door at the top and waiting for the wealth to trickle down, it would be cheaper and easier to offer the women cleaning the desks in banks, large companies and parliaments around the world a little more.

The rhetoric around work barely touches upon the realities of low pay. For all the lip service paid to "hard-working families", families on minimum wage, who need benefits in the UK or food stamps in the US, are an unspoken of class. Karolina, a young mother of two in Liverpool, sat with her beaming and wriggling six month-old son in her pristine front room, and explained the never-ending arithmetic that goes into ensuring the family can survive: "[My husband's] on minimum wage, full time. But he's doing overtime, because I'm on maternity leave, and last week he did 74 hours. It costs our family life, we hardly see him. And you don't even see the money because he pays more tax on it." The second her husband earns a little more, they receive a little less in housing benefit and working tax credits: government handouts that directly subsidise employers paying poverty wages. With overtime sporadic, he works more hours when he can, but the extra hours bring in negligible financial benefit. In the meantime, his children, a four year-old girl who has just started school and the six month-old baby, are rapidly growing and changing while he works every day of the week, leaving before they're awake, and returning home when they're already dreaming in bed.

For all the political and media insistence that a vast class of people in the UK and US choose surviving on welfare as a "lifestyle" and enjoy doing so, few people feel that way. As Karolina told me, "I would rather just take money from work, than the government. I've never been on jobseekers' once. And if I had a choice, I'd always rather work." The rhetoric around "welfare scroungers" is subtly gendered too: women are more likely to be economically inactive and therefore dependent on at least some state assistance for one simple reason: care. The bulk of care is still done by women, and remains unpaid, because gendered jobs are still undervalued. Couldn't making a proactive decision to value women's work be a solution?

One government did precisely this, recently—Yanis Varoufakis, the Greek finance minister, announced when his left-wing Syriza party came into power this year that they were cancelling the scheduled redundancies of the parliament's cleaners, and finding the money by firing some of the many financial advisers the previous government had hired. Rather than encouraging women to "lean in" and combat the drastic drop in earnings millions of Greek households had suffered, the Greek government chose to send a message that the women's work was more valuable than the almost exclusively male financial advisers. There's a poetry to the move that is deliberate: the global financial crisis was caused not by cleaners, low-paid workers, the poor, disabled or marginalised, but by widespread financial speculation, rigging and gambling by the very same people who remained in jobs. Taking a moral stand and signalling a sea change in the way work can be valued, and by extension people, is a small gesture, but one that could be replicated widely.

Pink Collars

A decade ago, I received a phone call offering me a part-time job in a nearby high-street chain store. Having sent in the application on a whim, with little expectation of success, it was a pleasant shock. My previous work experience amounted to Saturday jobs burning my hands on unwieldy coffee machines, and trying not to drop fried breakfasts while winding my way through scores of tables.

So the first day, with five other women being inducted, was a moment of tentative excitement. There was a uniform, a generous staff discount and a large staffroom upstairs. We were told, matter-of-factly, that we were all on "zero-hours contracts", though later we all confessed outside that we had no idea what that meant in practice.

We found out shortly afterwards. Each week, a staff rota was drawn up and displayed on the changing room noticeboard. Initially the shifts seemed to be regular, and shared relatively equally between all staff, with new employees given slightly fewer whilst completing training and learning the ropes. As the weeks wore on, the shop dynamic changed. I was polite and smart, and turned out to have a knack for selling shoes: one of the more involved shop-floor jobs, requiring a certain amount of cajoling, and measuring of customers' moods, trying to sound sincere while telling customers those patchwork knee-high boots were definitely flattering, and absolutely worth £80. But I was also able to respond positively to my manager's attempts to strike up conversation, in part due to nerves and a feeling that deference and amiability would elicit a positive response. I was quick to read her manner and second-guess what the subtext of her queries were; to guess when she was in a bad mood and offer support; to sense when she was stressed and offer help.

Other colleagues worked just as hard, but focussed less on this emotional labour. They were paid to do a certain task, so they'd do it well. Everything else was outside their remit. Another colleague enjoyed the job, but wasn't able to be as flexible with her hours, due to childcare issues. Finally, she called in sick, as her son was unwell and she had no luck finding a babysitter for the day. Despite the fact that the babysitter's fee would have rendered her shift financially pointless, after paying for travel, she recognised the need to appear keen and willing to work and tried to find a solution.

Slowly, these colleagues noticed their names cropping up

less and less often on the rotas, until they realised the reality of zero-hours contracts. Other staff members were hired, despite the fact that three or four colleagues were sat at home, wondering whether to take a chance on finding a new job. Nobody was ever fired. Instead they were slowly edged out, with no feedback on their performance, and no responsibility from management to fire them, left to realise slowly that they were effectively unemployed.

Ten years ago, zero-hours contracts weren't as common as they are now in Britain. Most part-time jobs offered you a minimum guarantee of hours, with the option of more overtime. The precarity of a zero-hours contract is well documented — when your employer can continue your employment with no guarantee of work, there's obviously no guarantee you can pay your rent. Even if your employer has not offered you work for weeks, you still can't quit and claim Jobseekers' Allowance in the UK, as the Department for Work and Pensions deems you to have made yourself deliberately unemployed.

The recession hastened this derision of employment rights. Seemingly overnight, workers in countries hit by the crash were told to be thankful they had a job at all. Especially for the lowest-paid workers, the message was clear that they should accept scraps from the table rather than demand their fair share of the bread. For my boss, and many others, this meant their role shifted from simply managing a small team in a straightforward manner, to an intense power play. To have a minimum-wage shift bestowed upon you, rearranging shirts by size order and tidying the shop floor wasn't enough. You had to perform for your manager, and engage in affective labour to curry favour and win rewards.

The psychological dynamics of workplaces run on zero-hours contracts are starkly different to salaried offices. Every colleague is competition. As a result you're constantly on edge, aware that the tiniest slip of the tongue or careless mistake could mean a fall from grace and attendant loss of income. In such circumstances, it's almost impossible to organise collectively. No one employed so precariously dare step out of line first, knowing the inevitable consequences. Such workplaces rarely recognise unions and actively discourage workers from joining or trying to form unions.

Instead, the workplace becomes more atomised, suspicion of colleagues higher, job satisfaction lower. Meanwhile the UK government wonders why productivity is so low: post-crash productivity has remained at roughly 16% below pre-crash levels. Ensuring your employees are kept in a state of precarity deskills your workforce. Productivity predictably slumps.

But the rise of precarity and attendant affective labour isn't confined to the lowest-paid sections of the workforce. Creative industries, and especially PR, expect extensive periods of free work, for which the unpaid are expected to be grateful, before even a sniff at a permanent contract. Much of the work involved in PR and publicity, "pink collar" jobs[33], revolves around the building of relationships. Relationships that are unlikely to be sincere, but require plenty of emotional labour regardless: the input is the same, and the attendant weariness and sting of rejection, and rebuffs from journalists, producers and clients has a high mental toll, as Jennifer Pan argues: "successful iterations of emotional labor require 'deep acting,' or a significant degree of identification with one's emotional performance. The constant negotiation between one's work role and one's own feelings that all emotional labor necessitates enacts a psychological toll on workers."[34] Women, "the softer sex", are expected to bear this emotional performance yet accept the fact that it is undervalued, both classified as an intrinsic skill that accompanies living whilst female, and the belief that it cannot be taught formally, so is less valuable.

This work, like low-paid retail work in which zero-hours contracts are common, is still predominantly carried out by women.

Eighty-five per cent of public-relations workers in the US are women[35], compared to 38% of the journalists they are paid to liaise with. As a result, it is undervalued, underpaid, and precarious. The psychological toll of being endlessly forced to perform emotional labour and project a workplace-mandated persona to yield results is underestimated and seen to be as valueless as it is unquantifiable. Heavy manual labour still retains an aura of "real work" due to its traditional industrial (male) connotations, whilst intellectual work is elevated to a far higher status than care, retail and menial labour, which is the preserve of women. Women's jobs are still not viewed as "proper" jobs outside of certain profession and income level: the assumption that women are earning pin money, or a secondary income, rather than fulfilling the role of breadwinner abdicates employers of the responsibility to take job satisfaction or skills seriously.

Anyone raising grievances with regard to their treatment is reminded that pink-collar jobs are competitive and desirable, in a cut-throat jobs market. The message is clear: in female-dominated industries and roles, workers are infinitely replaceable and of little value: if women aren't willing to work for a pittance without complaint, there are plenty more candidates willing and able to perform low-skill work.

In Joanna Biggs' recent book, *All Day Long: A Portrait of Britain at Work*[36], she profiles two baristas in a London branch of sandwich shop Pret a Manger. Pret a Manger prides itself on enforcing "The Pret Behaviours", listed in a book handed out to all staff, which explains that all staff must smile, try to chat to customers while their coffee is being prepared and act with the utmost enthusiasm at all times. Rather than receiving tips, bonuses are accrued based on the findings of Pret's mystery shoppers: with the bonus, an average worker's basic salary rises from £200 to £245.

Eighty per cent of mystery shoppers are happy, and the bonus is paid out. But it's indicative of a skewing of workplace dynamics and feelings about employees. Previously, if workers were unhappy in a workplace, the likelihood of strikes or workplace negotiations could improve conditions. Logic dictates that if workers are unhappy, making their working conditions and rewards more attractive will increase work satisfaction and therefore production.

But instead, corporations mandate happiness, making the performance a core skill of the job. Your happiness is no longer seen as an integral part of you, and contingent on outside forces, but instead a performative skill. Whether you're genuinely happy or not is irrelevant: but daring to show a flash of real emotion at work means knowing full well that your income and security is at risk.

Post-crash, the psychological power play between managers and the managed is more fraught than ever, with far more at stake. But employees, especially women, are no longer allowed to separate their working life from their personal life: monitoring of social media isn't uncommon, with tales abounding of people being sacked for thoughtless tweets or public Facebook posts. Much work now relies on emotional performance and projecting the impression that your working self is your whole self — the long-term implications for women are yet to be seen.

Money's Too Tight to Mention

People love money. Having money makes life in modern society far, far easier than not having money. The psychological stress of most jobs is less than the psychological stress of not being able to feed your children, or losing your home. But women's work is undervalued, as a whole (hence the gender pay-gap) and individually. Women are far less likely to ask for a pay rise, to put themselves forward for a promotion, or to negotiate their salary. Partly this is because of the way work is set up: to make discussion of money as difficult as possible. Staff are not likely to march into an office and ask for a pay cut, so it makes financial sense for a business to put off talk on pay, for fear of having to shell out more. The Chartered Institute of Managers found that Britons were more comfortable ending a relationship than discussing pay with their bosses. And this discomfort increases with gender: men apply for jobs if they fulfil some of the criteria, whereas most women will discount a job advert if they don't meet all of the requirements.

The secrecy around pay also locks women into lower-paid roles: many companies have clauses that stop employees from discussing pay. Even companies that have public pay scales will refuse to be drawn on which spine in the scale individuals are on, advertising bands instead of exact salaries. Two colleagues doing the same job could easily be paid a difference amounting to thousands of pounds.

At the same time as casual and precarious employment has increased dramatically, legal aid in England has effectively been removed; the cuts are so deep and the barriers so impermeable. Women wishing to take their employer to court for unfair dismissal, sexual harassment, bullying, or withheld pay must now pay tribunal fees of up to £1200 before the case can be heard. For many low-paid women, those who are most likely to be unfairly dismissed, this is completely unaffordable: all an unscrupulous employer needs to do to avoid a tribunal is withhold pay. In that case it's a win-win scenario: no legal hassle, as your former employee cannot afford to take you to task, and a small financial sweetener to boot.

Research from the Citizens' Advice Bureau pointed out the predictably catastrophic effect: 7 out of 10 legitimate grievances were now not being heard because of lack of funds on the part of the complainant.[37] The coalition lauded the vertiginous drop in tribunal figures as a triumph in the war on "false cases" rather than a wholesale stripping of rights from the poorest in society. Victim-blaming is abhorrent wherever it rears its head, but applauding the fact that thousands are denied justice, and a snide assertion that the reason it was high before was because women are liars, is reprehensible.

The argument for introducing tribunal fees also claims that tribunals were hurting small, struggling businesses. The idea that hordes of unscrupulous women were roaming the country, looking for jobs they could secure long enough to bring a tribunal, is laughable. Pursuing and sitting through a tribunal is a massive upheaval that no one takes on lightly or without a reasonable prospect of winning. If, as the government claims, a small number of people brought tribunals falsely, they have bigger problems than a sheaf of court admin to wade through. Most of these women aren't working for small firms: they're outsourced cleaners working in big corporation buildings, cleaning banks, Parliament, multinationals.

The Birmingham cleaners (see Chapter 1) would struggle today to bring their case to court, because of their relative poverty: because they decided to collectively lean out and fight their employers in a long and hard battle, they secured a victory and justice for the work they had carried out and been underpaid for. No amount of leaning in and continuing to collude with a system that was so deliberately designed to reward men to the detriment of women would have secured the same result.

CHAPTER 5

Trickledown Feminism

"Someone once said that it is easier to imagine the end of the world than to imagine the end of capitalism. We can now revise that and witness the attempt to imagine capitalism by way of imagining the end of the world." — FREDERIC JAMESON

The central argument of 1% feminism—that getting women into high positions is better for everyone, because feminism "trickles down" and becomes the norm—works about as well as trickledown economics. Women in high positions are still fundamentally part of the business world, and business institutions by and large favour wealth-hoarding over greater equality. Business perpetuates oppressive social structures, rather than subverting them. The aim of business is to generate profit and capital, not pour oil over society's ills, but to profit from anything possible.

In the past 10 years, the wealth of the super-rich has soared, while the poorest are poorer than ever. To qualify as a member of the super-rich and make it into such hallowed yet nauseating publications as *The Sunday Times Rich List* requires an income of around £43 million in the UK, to reach around number 200. High pay is rarely queried seriously in the media, and far less than the amount received by those on benefits in the UK has been. Danny Dorling points out: "If National Wage had kept pace with FTSE 100 CEO salaries since 1999, it would now stand at £18.89 per hour".[38] Of course, it hasn't. Even in the 2015 budget, when it was announced the minimum wage would rise to £7.20 in April 2016, George Osborne cynically rebranded it a "living wage". The Living Wage, an actual calculated hourly rate for a minimum standard of living, is higher

(£9.15 in London, £7.85 everywhere else[39]), as the Living Wage Campaign was quick to point out. But the theft of the term and its false application is difficult to claw back, and in doing so, Osborne effectively silenced calls for higher minimum wages that are actually liveable.

Meanwhile, more women have become billionaires, and entered the super-rich. Ultimately, the entry of women into the world's 1% is depicted as progress—but the wealth hoarding of the super-rich has catastrophic effects for everyone further down the chain, especially women. The feminism of the 1% asks that the appointment of any woman to a high-powered job be treated as a victory for women as a whole, without examining whether it genuinely has any wider effect on society.

"This is state-sanctioned abuse of women"

The notorious Yarl's Wood detention centre was opened in 2001, under the last Labour government, and management was outsourced to private company Serco in 2007. Poor conditions in the centre and protests against the 400-capacity facility have intensified in recent years, coming to a head in 2015. Reports of sexual abuse and mistreatment in the compound became increasingly common, and self-harm was rife among the women, who comprised of failed asylum seekers awaiting deportation, imprisoned despite committing no crime. A Channel 4 investigation obtained footage of the systemic mistreatment of women detained in the centre, included a guard shouting "Headbutt the bitch. I'd beat her up."[40]

Rashida Manjoo, the United Nation's special rapporteur on violence against women, was barred from Yarl's Wood by the Home Office in April 2014[41] when she tried to investigate complaints as part of her fact-finding mission into violence against women in the UK. Cameras have never been allowed in. In April 2015, in the same week as a woman died in Yarl's Wood and a guard with a history of sexually inappropriate behaviour was suspended pending investigation for a revenge assault, Cristel Amiss, of the Black Women's Rape Action Project, told *The Guardian*: "We've been supporting women in Yarl's Wood for over a decade and have heard consistent reports from brave whistleblowers exposing abusive treatment and sexually predatory behaviour by guards."[42]

After the Channel 4 investigation, Theresa May refused to come to the House of Commons to answer an urgent question from the Shadow Home Secretary, Yvette Cooper, on the treatment of detainees, called amongst other abusive names "black bitch", "animals", "beasties", and "evil".[43] Cooper said, "There is no point in ministers pretending to be shocked at news of abuse. This is not news. Even now, the ministers have not set up an independent inquiry. This is state-sanctioned abuse of women on the Home Secretary's watch and it needs to end now."

Despite May's assertions that she believes in women's empowerment, there is a distinct limit to her solidarity, which depends on how your race, country of birth, and economic wealth intersect. As Home Secretary, May is in a position rarely occupied by women, and rarely occupied by anyone for so long. Home Secretaries tend to be hit by scandals and forced to resign with wearying regularity. But whilst in office, May has overseen some of the most draconian immigration legislation for decades, defending immigration detention, renewing contracts with Serco despite sexual violence reports, and introducing rules that mean low income families are split up and British people split up from their partners and children if they don't earn over a soon-to-be-raised income threshold.

May sits in a cabinet with many other powerful women, especially after criticism of Cameron's disproportionately male and Etonian cabinet refused to die down until a reshuffle. The policies that trickle down from that cabinet harm women disproportionately. Despite launching a campaign titled "Theresa May for Equal Pay".[44] in 2008, May has endorsed an austerity regime that saw the gender pay-gap increase, and been a stalwart of a government that introduced cuts that affected four times as many women as men.

Meanwhile, there is a burgeoning crisis in the women's sector: provision of domestic violence services and rape crisis centres and helplines has been reduced due to austerity cuts. Headline figures on cuts to UK domestic violence services often mask the full impact of government cuts on people fleeing abuse at home. Women across the UK have been hardest hit by austerity and attendant spending cuts.[45] Charities in the sector speak out about the problems they're seeing: Women's Aid has warned that services are "at breaking point"[46], with a third of women turned away from refuges due to lack of space, and the total number of refuges falling from 187 to 155 between 2010 and 2014.[47] But for many of the women escaping violence, moving to a refuge is only the first step on the journey to safe, independent living.

The housing crisis, especially in the south east and London, is one of the biggest factors affecting women trying to move on. Most women spend between six to nine months in refuges, where they're assigned a support worker who offers counselling, signposts services and advocates for the women, helping them build independent living skills, and getting them into education and training. The move to independence after surviving violence is crucial, as without support and safeguards put in place, the risk of returning home to violence and abuse is heightened.

At one refuge in London last year, run by the charity Hestia, the service manager Louise Dickerson told me: "It's really difficult in the climate now. Because social housing is pretty much abolished, local authorities discharge their duty through private rented accommodation now most often, which is maybe on a yearly license or tenancy." Housing waiting lists in the UK's local councils, who have a legal duty to help homeless and vulnerable people, are at an all-time high. With so much pressure on councils, domestic violence survivors can struggle to convince council employees they are a priority. Women have even spoken of being disbelieved when they disclose their need to flee because of violence. Moving to privately rented flats means the women and families are offered less security and are liable for far higher rents: most private housing offers tenancy agreements of no longer than a year, and Hestia report more women are being asked to have a financial guarantor, who agrees to be financially liable for rent arrears. For women fleeing violence, who've often cut all ties to their wider family and friendship groups, this is an impossibility and an insult after their ordeal.

Even when women do find a home to move on to, the cuts mean they face even more hardship. In the raft of public-spending cuts in the last few years, many of the financial assistance schemes councils offered have been slashed. The crisis loan fund, which provided a total of £180m in hardship loans to people in extreme financial need, has now been scrapped. Economic control is a commonly used tool of domestic violence perpetrators when preventing women from leaving: removing financial help for such vulnerable women and children puts lives at risk. This money was previously a lifeline for people in extreme distress and very vulnerable situations, and losing it puts even more pressure on domestic violence services. As Dickerson explains:

> They've taken away the crisis loan, and women relied on that for resettlement. So women will leave without a mattress to sleep on, and some of them have young families. One woman was self-harming recently, living in a shelter that was not homely. It's very challenging for our workers. We work really hard just to make sure the women can survive.

Other lifelines of financial support are also being slowly eroded. The Discretionary Housing Payment funding, which provides payments of up to a year for people facing difficulty paying their accommodation costs, is to be slashed by 24% from 2015.

In a speech to Women's Aid's annual conference in 2010 in the early days of the coalition, May told the audience that both the Conservatives and the Liberal Democrats would reverse the decline in rape crisis centres, but tentatively refused to make any funding commitments to the women's sector in the face of looming local authority cuts. "Your problem is my problem", May said, adding, "Success for us will not mean we've spent more of the money we don't have. It will mean more women have been helped, more abusers have been brought to justice and more attitudes have been changed."

It's not precisely clear how May and the government expect rape crisis centres to continue to provide an identical service with less money, which perhaps explains why she is not chancellor, but does little to comfort the women in need who find their service threatened with closure. Violence against women is a problem for all of society, and without accepting that all services must be welcoming and accessible for women fleeing violence and crucially that they must be adequately funded, more women will find their lives in danger.

The benefit of having women in the cabinet remains to be seen for migrant, low-paid, or abused women. For now, it seems as though there is no difference: the powerful look after the powerful, with gender as an afterthought, or a bargaining chip when trying to deflect criticism for cuts that harm women.

The idea that getting more women into positions of power automatically benefits women as a whole seems logical, but curtly overlooks competing interests of class, race, and social and economic position. Whilst parliaments and cabinets continue to be predominantly white, male, pale, and stale, those women who do elbow their way in tend not to be the acutely underrepresented, but those who fit into a similar culture. The Conservative's portrait of Margaret Thatcher, a lowly daughter of a greengrocer, crucially misrepresents the fact that she was a university-educated barrister, and her father was less a grocer, more an entrepreneur and business owner.

By the time Margaret Thatcher was born in 1925, Alfred Roberts owned two grocers' shops in Grantham. He was also, according to biographer Bernard Crick, a prolific groper, harassing many young women and girls employed in his shops. This fact was an open secret in Grantham, with many people discouraging girls from taking jobs in his shops. When this information was passed to a *Daily Mirror* journalist shortly before the 1987 general election, they declined to publish the story. The Conservatives were also aware of the allegations, Crick says[48], and fully aware of how damaging this would be whilst promoting "family values". Roberts' position in the community as a lay preacher, businessman, and politician protected him, while the women assaulted were denied justice, as the story remained out of the press until shortly after the 1997 general election.

Decades later, a familiar tale emerges, of powerful men permitted to rape, sexually assault, and grope women, girls and boys with impunity, due to their political, social and economic power. The state was aware of the allegations, and decided it was politically expedient to ignore and by extension condone these crimes. A roll call of politicians and senior figures involved in sexual abuse from the 1970s onwards could double as Margaret Thatcher's address book.

Rumours abounded for years about the crimes and proclivities of Jimmy Savile, but UK libel law, a protective elite, and his own powerful reputation meant the allegations were confined to rumour, either slipped into broadcasts and articles through subterfuge in complex and intricate metaphors and couching of phrases, or residing in the more obscure and discredited home of conspiracy theorists, David Icke's website. Savile's victims were predominantly condemned to vulnerability by both their gender and class. If females and the economic underclass are seen as less human, when the two intersect society for the most part scorns them.

But evidence has emerged that Margaret Thatcher was aware of the ongoing abuses by the fellow members of the political and cultural elite. An undated letter sent from Lord Shackleton of the political honours scrutiny committee to Thatcher, and marked "secret", warned that conferring an honour on Rochdale MP Cyril Smith "could give rise to adverse criticism", due to reports in *Private Eye* and the Rochdale Press that he had abused several young boys. Cyril Smith was knighted in 1988.

At Stoke Mandeville hospital, Jimmy Savile's reputation and fundraising success gave him free rein to rape and assault children, as young as eight, for years. Children reporting rape were chastised by nurses and ordered to keep quiet. One girl was reprimanded and reminded of how much money he made for the children's hospital. In 1980, Savile became the lead fundraiser and commissioning project manager for the hospital's £10m campaign to rebuild the spinal injuries unit. The move, which gave him "virtually uncontested authority and control"[49], was endorsed by Thatcher.

Throughout her time in power, Thatcher repeatedly lobbied for Savile to be knighted. Her efforts were rebuffed, with concerns over his "manner of life" and "lurid details" about his sexual life. In 1983, Sir Robert Armstrong wrote to Thatcher to express concern about these perpetual requests, warning "fears have been expressed that Mr. Savile might not be able to refrain from exploiting a knighthood in a way which brought the honours system into disrepute".[50] Thatcher continued to press for Savile's knighthood, which was eventually conferred shortly after she left office in 1990.

After his death, when details of his permitted crimes were revealed to the public, there were widespread calls for his knighthood to be rescinded. The Cabinet Office replied that honours ceased to exist in effect upon death, so rescinding his knighthood was impossible. In life, his benevolent public face was upheld, in part due to the most powerful woman in Britain.

Thatcher's role in ensuring Savile's untouchability, alongside numerous other powerful rapists and paedophiles, shows she was no friend to women. The economic and social devastation wrought upon working-class communities and industries also hit women far harder than men. But the fact of her power and her gender emboldens 1% feminists to claim her as a feminist icon, purely by virtue of her sex and in spite of the fact she was clearly not an advocate of women's social and economic empowerment. There is no intrinsic tendency for women to support other women when competing class and power interests offer far more fruitful personal rewards.

This class divide in the value of women's lives is echoed in the treatment of girls in the Rochdale and Oxford grooming scandals. Whilst many newspapers and reports focussed on the race of the majority of charged perpetrators, little attention was paid to the fact that it was the girls' vulnerability that enabled their attackers to first find them, then continually abuse them unhindered by any authority. Official inquiries into the abuse scandals showed a rotten system that treated the girls not as second-class citizens, but as barely human. Social workers, police, councillors all acted as though the drug addictions the girls presented with were an inevitable consequence of being a working-class girl in care, and that rather than being groomed, raped, and forced to sleep with complete strangers, the girls were entering into these situations willingly.

That their lives had taken this turn was not seen as abuse, but a natural path. For all the talk of a sexual liberation for women in the 21st century, conceptions of female sexuality are still mired in throwback ideas around class. Middle-class and wealthier women have glossy, empowering sex that is liberating in its promiscuity, whereas working-class women fuck like unevolved bovine creatures. While the middle class "have children", the working class, especially those on benefits, "breed", if poisonous tabloid invective is to be believed.

For these women, getting more women into power had a negligible effect on their life, since austerity and cuts to services, and the mechanisms that scrutinised those services, left them vulnerable. The idea that women will work in favour of women wherever they are in business or politics simply doesn't pan out, and remains insulting to women. The imagined solidarity between women of all ages, classes, and social backgrounds simply doesn't exist. Expecting women of disparate social status to hold their breath while forcing in a few women at the top, and hoping the benefits trickle down to their level at some point, is as patronising as it is opportunist for wealthy and more privileged women.

CHAPTER 6

Can You Be a Feminist and ...?

"All my lousy life I've crawled about in the mud! And you talk to me about scenery!" — SAMUEL BECKETT, *Waiting for Godot*

Media narratives around feminism have become more embracing of the term. At the same time, a fixation has grown around how many women (and increasingly men) "define as feminist" without exploring what constitutes feminism. Annual think pieces declaring a "new wave" of feminist activism appear to rehash the same claim that suddenly feminism has become mainstream, focussing on one or two small, usually white and middle-class, campaigns.

Concurrently, the rise of "choice feminism" is seen in opinion pieces from female writers — the refrain "Can you be a feminist and...?" prefaces almost every life choice women can purportedly make. A list from a cursory search includes:

Can you be a feminist and...
drink milk?
be a fashion lover?
wear high heels?
put your hands on your hips?
have a boob job?
hate your body?
work for a lads' mag?
vajazzle?

Choice feminism treats the movement as another aspect of an individual's "lifestyle". Asking "Can you be a feminist and?" posits a political position as just another facet of modern contemporary life. Can you be an investment banker and do yoga? Can you be a soldier and eat crisps? None of the individual choices are feminist: but choice feminism, like Sandberg's corporate feminism, maintains an inward-looking and insular view of what feminism can and should be. Part of the problem with choice feminism remains the fact that following through the argument, it is up to individual women to act in a manner befitting feminism: the goals and battles of the feminist movement will then fall into place.

The reduction of feminism to individual women's choices, often bound up in consumer culture stymies, attempts to move the critical lens from women's collective position in society to an individualist level. This tallies with Sandberg's central premise: that women's behaviour, rather than patriarchal power structures in work and society, is what causes gender inequality and is holding women back. Repackaging feminism as a lifestyle choice, rather than a political movement demanding change, becomes inward-looking.

The rise of consumerist hijacking of feminism (Fawcett/ Whistles t-shirts, "Feminist" necklaces, etc.) whitewashes brands and corporations' complicity in the economic structures that perpetuate inequality, while also often relying on low-cost female labour in sweatshops abroad and precarious contracts in the West. "Lifestyle feminism" also privileges consumption over action, and by extension depicts white, middle-class feminism as the dominant and default. For women struggling to meet basic needs, discussions over whether or not one can be feminist and wear high heels are of no consequence to their material existence, ignoring poverty, labour, and reproductive rights.

Branding Feminism

Liberation movements often become co-opted by multinationals and big business at precisely the moment when it becomes politically expedient to do so. The most nakedly opportunistic example of this is Google's decision to release a rainbow "doodle" to coincide with the Sochi Winter Olympics in Russia in 2014. As Emily Greenhouse notes in *The New Yorker*:

> In 2008, Google's co-founder, Sergey Brin, took to the official Google blog to voice the company's support for marriage equality during California's legal battle over the Proposition 8 ballot measure. But it wasn't until February of this year, on the day of the opening ceremony in Sochi, that Google made a broader show of support for gay rights, by displaying a rainbow-backed homepage logo depicting six athletes engaged in Winter Olympic events. Google's doodle, visible worldwide, marked a clear objection to Russia's homophobic law banning "propaganda of nontraditional sexual relations to minors." That move dovetailed with the opening up of gay-rights attitudes in many countries. (A Pew Research Center survey last year found "broad acceptance of homosexuality in North America, the European Union, and much of Latin America, but equally widespread rejection in predominantly Muslim nations and in Africa, as well as in parts of Asia and in Russia.") [51]

Similarly, Honeymaid and Coca-Cola have endeavoured to insert fleeting glimpses of same-sex families in their advertising, now that it tests well with the market. This doesn't function as a bold political move that risks alienating a broad percentage of their consumers—instead it gives the companies the opportunity to appear "liberal" in a society that is predominantly accepting of the fact that heterosexuality isn't the only relationship model. Likewise, corporate feminism is as business-friendly and as unthreatening as the capitalist system could hope for—the focus on how you can "have it all" inevitably means: be the best worker a company could hope for.

Perhaps the most nakedly opportunistic example of a brand co-opting feminism is Dove's campaign. The soap and moisturiser pedlar has for years now championed "real women" through targeted advertising campaigns professing their scented bottles of unguent are for "everyone" rather than just models. A more recent campaign featured a short film of women describing how they looked while a forensic artist sketched a composite of their face, then being shown a drawing based on another person's description of them. The advert went viral, as cod-affirmative mawkish clips by professional ad-men often do. As Arwa Mahdawi wrote in *The Guardian*, Dove "has mastered the art of passing off somewhat passive-aggressive and patronising advertising as super-empowering, ultra PR-able social commentary." [52] Dove, like many other companies, hasn't suddenly grown a conscience in the depths of Unilever's offices, but instead spotted a new avenue for aggressive selling, and commandeered it.

Wider access to the internet and the exponential growth and diversification of social media has spawned the opportunity to create spaces for far-flung but similar people to share things that interest each other, converse, read, and learn. The growth of Tumblr is in part down to an army of teenagers and young women sharing and commenting on things they enjoy: political notes, videos, and photographs that they find comforting, validating, and nourishing. These tend to be about social justice, personal lives, lifestyles, and body image. Wherever there is an organic space for individuals to read, connect, and spend time, companies will see an opportunity for marketing.

That feminism has become an attractive marketing tool is a progress of sorts. Wider public acceptance of the fact that, actually, women might possibly be human and deserve to live unhindered by violence, damaging preconceptions, and systemic barriers in life, is not to be baulked at. But hijacking by brands will always water down radical political movements, and distil them into reductive definitions that end up doing more harm than good. If a brand or large organisation wants to commandeer a feminist cause, it is definitely not due to the fact a corporate capitalist entity has decided to shift focus from money-making to philanthropy and engineering social change.

For years, countries intent on military aggression and Islamophobic groups have engaged in "pink-washing" — the appropriation of gay rights to bolster their own image as modern, inclusive, and benevolent, whilst attacking Muslim countries and communities, depicted as backwards and hateful. Pink-washing ignores the experience of Muslim and minority gay and lesbian lives, fully endorsing a narrow and limited view of how Muslims live, think, and feel, in favour of stereotypes that supposedly justify their hate.

Israel has been a particular proponent of pink-washing, publicising gay-pride marches as a marketing strategy, all the while bombing Palestine, and when the fatalities are met with global outcry, arguing that those killed are a dangerous people, homophobic, anti-semitic, and heavily invested in the oppression of women. That doesn't explain why, with some of the world's most targeted and sophisticated missiles, the oppressors they kill are children playing on beaches near hotels, or civilians huddling in UN schools. To anyone willing to spend more than five minutes considering the situation, it looks far more like an oppressive and wealthy regime starving people in an open prison, ramping up settlement building whilst claiming those imprisoned and denied land, provisions, and the opportunity to live free of fear are actually the oppressors.

Sarah Schulman writes in *The New York Times*:

In 2005, with help from American marketing executives, the Israeli government began a marketing campaign, "Brand Israel," aimed at men ages 18 to 34. The campaign, as reported by *The Jewish Daily Forward*, sought to depict Israel as "relevant and modern." The government later expanded the marketing plan by harnessing the gay community to reposition its global image.[53]

Image is important when the actions you are undertaking are violent, or morally indefensible. As with pink-washing, the incursion into Afghanistan by American and allied troops from 2001 onwards co-opted a liberation movement's rhetoric to justify military force and invasion. In November 2001, both First Lady Laura Bush and Prime Minister's wife Cherie Blair spoke on the plight of women and children in Afghanistan, underlining that the war was a humanitarian endeavour, with feminist principles. I don't define both women by their husbands' roles carelessly: Bush was a former librarian, and Blair a prominent barrister and jurist, but their speeches were stage-managed to add weight to the narrative that the US and UK incursion had the interests of oppressed women at heart and wasn't purely a badly planned retaliation for the September 11th atrocities. War is macho, and bloody: trying to soften it by co-opting feminism to justify the cost and attendant death needs female voices to add weight to such a flimsy claim.

Imperialist feminism has a long history, as Katharine Viner points out, with the rescue of the vulnerable (read: women and children) white-washing more insidious motives for invasion, war and colonisation:

> The Victorian male establishment, which led the great imperialistic ventures of the 19th century, fought bitterly against women's increasingly vocal feminist demands and occasional successes (a handful going to university; new laws permitting married women to own property); but at the same time, across the globe, they used the language of feminism to acquire the booty of the colonies.[54]

One of these Victorian males, Lord Cromer was particularly keen that veiled Egyptian women should de-jab, arguing that Islam's monstrous mistreatment of women was holding Egypt back from entering the enlightened and idealised version of

Western civilisation that bastion of women's rights Cromer claimed to inhabit. Back home, Cromer was the founder and head of the Men's League for Opposing Women's Suffrage. Women's rights are a handy garnish of conscience in foreign policy, but domestic policy is a different issue. Bush wasted no time in blocking abortion rights in his first term in office, but was happy to co-opt feminist concern and a false narrative of female emancipation to justify a lengthy and catastrophic war. As Viner says:

> Feminism is used for everything these days, except the fight for true equality — to sell trainers, to justify body mutilations, to make women make porn, to help men get off rape charges, to ensure women feel they have self-respect because they use a self-esteem-enhancing brand of shampoo. No wonder it's being used as a reason for bombing women and children too.[55]

Individualist Feminism

Despite regularly being told feminism is having a resurgence, which to older feminists rightly makes them wonder exactly when it went away, this often amounts to little more than a few opinion pieces in a handful of online outlets. What's on offer isn't wildly exciting: predominantly a litany of articles that focus on whether individual choices, hobbies, or proclivities are "feminist". "Can you be a feminist and?" articles invariably answer "yes" to a question almost nobody was asking. They speak of a feminism that is inward-looking, and focus on individual identity rather than collective emancipation. The language of liberation and emancipation is often attached to consumerist choices, such as wearing make-up, buying clothes, or having plastic surgery.

Choice feminism states that any choice is feminist purely by virtue of having been made by a woman: that she is in a position to, and has, made a choice is thereby feminist. There's little analysis paid to what this means for women in society as a whole, or how some choices (such as deciding to rescind abortion rights when in political office, or choosing to deny your partner the right to leave the house) obviously don't act in the interest of feminism. Self-acceptance and whether something is "individually empowering" replace demands for constructive, structural, political, and economic change.

Choice feminism turns feminism into a lifestyle rather than a radical emancipatory politics. A vision of feminism preoccupied with what feminism can do for one person's individual life immediately, as Nina Power neatly argues:

> Stripped of any internationalist and political quality, feminism becomes about as radical as a diamante phone cover. [Jessica] Valenti "truly believes" that feminism is necessary for women "to live happy fulfilled lives". Slipping down as easily as a friendly-bacteria yoghurt drink, Valenti's version of feminism, with its total lack of structural analysis, genuine outrage or collective demand, believes it has to complement capitalism in order to effectively sell its product.[56]

The problem with feminism is that the demand for radical and collective action and structural change will never sit well with capitalism. As a lifestyle, feminism can only work if it doesn't challenge, and instead works within, traditional power structures, be they political or commerce-oriented.

Obsession with lifestyle — whether aspects of mainstream culture are feminist — turns attention back on the self rather than women's position in society and attendant life chances. As Linda R. Hirschman puts it:

> "Choice feminism", the shadowy remnant of the original movement, tells women that their choices, everyone's choices, the incredibly constrained "choices" they make, are good

choices. Everyone says if feminism failed it was because it was too radical. But we know — and surely the real radical, Betty Friedan, knew — that it wasn't because feminism was too radical. It was because feminism wasn't radical enough. A movement that stands for everything ultimately stands for nothing.[57]

One can care about more than one issue at a time, and everybody does. But media coverage is still only as finite as the reporters covering a story, and the intensity of coverage of some issues is inevitably at the cost of others. Take, for instance, the furore over adverts by Protein World on the London Underground, showing an extremely slim woman in a bikini under the slogan "Are you beach body ready?" The campaign against the adverts grew quickly, predominantly on social media, with the inevitable flash mob, and countless online articles lobbying for the adverts to be removed sprang up.

A petition to remove the adverts garnered 71,111 signatures in a short period. At the current time, a petition for the Conservative government to remove the "rape test" on child benefit claims for third children has received 1,604. Time and attention within life are finite, and "wins" that seem more achievable are more likely to spur the column inches which are then denied to issues that hit the invisible, the poorer, and the more marginalised.

An obsession with lifestyle also obscures the fact that for huge numbers of women, problems in life aren't related to being upset about images in magazines, mulling over whether high heels are a symbol of the patriarchy, or whether you can enjoy being spanked and still be a feminist. They're economic, because economics is a feminist issue. As with banking, many politicians and facets of the media have wilfully obfuscated on issues around the economy: when the financial crash happened, we were told the banking system was far too complex for mere mortals to understand, so whatever you do, don't attempt to scrutinise any of the actions that led to the crash. It's the same for economics, and there's a gender aspect here based on who studies what: economics, like maths and science, has always been seen as a hard science, and traditionally male. Implying that even the most basic mechanisms of the economy are highly technical and inscrutable for a layperson is a helpful message to disseminate when austerity hits women so hard, yet is still built on a shaky, if non-existent, evidence base.

Feminism based on lifestyle assumes that feminism is a middle-class concern. The obsession with whether or not women identify as feminists assumes that this is a reasonable measure of how many people believe in the general aims and objectives of the ideology. But it is a preoccupation that relies on identity labels more than any analysis of shared values. And any identity can and will be co-opted for political gain: hence we see Nick Clegg, the former Deputy Prime Minister, and former leader of the Liberal Democrats, posing in a "This is what a feminist looks like" t-shirt despite having signed a Faustian pact for a sniff at power, and enabling the cuts that saw women's economic position attacked on every level for five years. Meanwhile, David Cameron was chastised for refusing to wear one, as if a t-shirt sent from Whistles could absolve him of all his policy sins. Whether or not someone embraces the feminist label is a moot point in the end, as Zoe Williams points out:

> People who like to sound the death knell for the ideology – it's remarkable even that such people still exist – point to the fact that young women tend not to describe themselves as feminists. There is a certain sour enjoyment from pointing out all the privileges that they owe to the sisterhood – the equal pay, the maternity leave – but I would query the importance of the self-description. One can promulgate the values of feminism quite effectively by just living them, by expecting fairness at work and at home, and young women are better at this, less surrendered, than anyone.[58]

The crowing denunciation of those who wouldn't call themselves feminist carries an implicit snobbery. You idiot! Don't you like the idea of equal pay? And of course, most women wouldn't argue against the opportunity to close the gender pay-gap. But when media feminism seems dominated by lifestyle choices and narrowly focused on individual consumerism, it's difficult to see how such a label can make a difference to your everyday life.

Working-Class Feminism

Working-class feminism exists outside of most media narratives, but is far harder to write a chirpy feature about because, like most aspects of working-class life, it becomes enmeshed in many other axes of oppression: class, disability, age, region, race, education all bind together to affect a person's life chances, and compound day-to-day discrimination. For working-class women, simply being a feminist isn't enough to cover the myriad hardships enacted upon them and their peers. Life isn't so simple. But a tendency to decry women who either eschew the "feminist" label, or simply not to identify with it, oversimplifies feminist aims and ideas, whilst implying that those who when asked would shrug or baulk at the identity label are uneducated, or put off by politics because they're simply too intimidated by big ideas.

Real life examples show, of course, that this isn't the case, and that working-class feminist activism and anger is palpable and widespread. "People will always judge you when you've got two kids and no job", Donna, a 21 year-old single mother tells me in Brixton Library one afternoon. "Especially because my eldest is mixed [race]. You can see their faces making up ideas about you before you've barely said anything. And they're like 'Well why did you have kids then?' but they're here now, so now what?" Donna's point chimes with much of the discussion of the working class, and especially working-class women, in the media.

Poverty, we're told by our political betters, is a result of laziness and a dereliction of "aspiration".[59] In 2013, Mick Philpott was convicted of starting a house fire that killed six children, five of whom he had fathered. *The Daily Mail's* front page following the conviction of Mick Philpott, a photo of Philpott with some of his children, emblazoned with the headline "Vile Product of Welfare UK" provoked outrage for making a cheap political point from the death of six children. *The Mail* and many other papers paid little attention to the other female victims of Philpott: the court case revealed he had an extreme history of physical and sexual violence and had systematically attacked and controlled his partners. The house fire was started as a ruse to frame the children's mother, Philpott's partner, for the arson after she had dared to leave him. But this headline was merely the culmination of years of vilification and monstering of the British underclass, at the hands of politicians and the media, keen to use the welfare system as an easy target to score approval points amongst voters.

Much of the debate around reproductive rights centres on the right to abortion and the affordability of childcare. Increasingly, media and political narratives have singled out women like Donna, and any families who choose to have children on low incomes.

For many working-class people, the poisonous invective against "dependency culture" leaves them fighting to justify their existence, and their right to start a family. Working-class female sexuality is similarly depicted as bovine and boorish, the "wrong" kind of promiscuity, while a glitzier, posher sexuality, bound up in consumerism, is sold to us constantly through the media as liberation.

In 2013, the IPPR published research into feminism and class and how many working-class women felt feminism had failed them.[59] Dalia Ben-Galim, the IPPR's associate director, said:

While feminism has delivered for some professional women, other women have been left behind. Many of the advances for women at the top have masked inequality at the bottom. The "break the glass ceiling" approach that simply promotes women in the boardroom has not been as successful in changing family-friendly working culture or providing opportunities for other women to advance. Gender still has a strong independent impact on women's earnings prospects – but class, education and occupational backgrounds are stronger determinants of a woman's progression and earnings prospects.[61]

Higher education has a much higher impact on raising pay for women than men—as the IPPR report points out—and this is borne out in how pay and quality of life have improved dramatically for middle-class women, in a way that has been markedly slower for working-class women.

And austerity is an intrinsically gendered issue.[62] It hits women far harder than men, as research repeatedly confirms.[63] Cuts to tax credits, caps on benefits, the introduction of the bedroom tax, the squeeze on jobs and wages, and pay cuts of 6% in real terms over the last five years[64] have hit women disproportionately, as the lowest earners and primary caregivers. The glass ceiling isn't absolute: the poorest women find their earning potential stalls at a far lower level than their university-educated and middle-class counterparts. And while cultural feminism may up click-rates on a headline, it is economics that affects women's lives day in, day out, stunting life chances and locking people into poverty.

The tendency to focus on vocal self-definition as a "feminist" has become a distraction, with campaigns to encourage those who don't self-identify as feminists to do so, whilst simultaneously overlooking ordinary women's concerns, and ignoring the work and campaigns these women are doing to fight back and improve their lot. The most publicised campaigns, as Lola

Okolosie points out, "do not reflect the most pressing needs of the majority of women, black and minority-ethnic women included. The problem is not that these campaigns exist, but that they are given a focus and attention that overshadows other work feminists are engaged with."[65] In the biannual lifestyle spreads on "the resurgence of feminism", there are often mentions of media-savvy campaigns, especially if they feature young, photogenic women in slogan t-shirts or costumes; but grassroots campaigns on benefits, low pay, housing, and childcare, campaigns that tend to attract working-class, older women, find their activities confined to the back pages of their local papers, if they don't upset the applecart too much.

An obsession with individualism and personal choice is costing the movement at large. The tired debate on "rebranding" feminism, personally identifying as a feminist, and pigeonholing different campaigns as "waves" smacks of a movement that prizes "awareness" over action. Lucy Mangan argues that "'Rebranding' – like all forms of marketing – is the ultimate in dickering about at the edges. It's so much easier than actually creating something whose worth people will come to recognise."[66] Much of the discourse around "rebranding" feminism focuses less on the universal problems that structural inequality causes, and more on, to borrow Rhian E Jones' words, reaching out to "the thick and theoryless"[67]: women who are mischaracterised as unenlightened and othered due to their class and socioeconomic position. The idea that there isn't a working-class feminist movement until it defines and speaks of itself in terms the middle class approves of is tiresome and reductive. The recession has caused a political resurgence amongst women in some of our poorest communities—people who for years were cowed by the media narrative that demonised them and bemoaned their very existence.

Many community campaigns against the cuts, or for better work and conditions, are led by women—women who are vocal, politically savvy, and have an understanding of economics informed by the fact that every aspect of their lives are under-pinned by the smallest cuts to benefits and wages. Talk of how feminism can "reach out" to women who are often active, but who don't consider their gender to be separate from their class, ethnicity, or economic status misses the point and condescends. Working-class feminism is alive and well, even if it doesn't focus on "brands" and selling an idea.

CHAPTER 7

Backlash

"There's no such thing as the voiceless, only the deliberately silenced and the preferably unheard." — ARUNDHATI ROY

Post-crash, countless studies have shown that the impact of cuts and austerity has been borne predominately by women. A Fawcett Society study on the impact of cuts doled out by the coalition government in the UK stated that 75% of all cuts hit women.[68] Women with disabilities, black women, working-class women, and single mothers were the hardest hit.

The Social Mobility and Child Poverty Commission warn that 2010–2020 will be the first decade since records began that sees a rise in absolute poverty in the UK, with the gulf between the rich and poor as irreparable.[69] When the economy tanks, it is predictably women who suffer. The fight for women's rights is less a long, slow march, and more like a climbing wall: it is possible to climb as well as fall, so vigilance is essential at all times. The clawing back of the welfare state is a direct attack on women's rights, but boardroom quotas make a tidier headline, based on the assumption that certain rights have already been won.

In reaction to the argument that "there is no alternative" to cuts and austerity, with Labour and the Conservatives in the UK singing from the same hymn sheets, women's grassroots groups have started to fight back. The Focus E15 campaign grew in Newham in response initially to Newham's "social cleansing" of the poorest households in the borough, targeting single mothers and forcing them to relocate to cities and towns hundreds of miles away from their children's schools, families and support networks. In 2013, a group of 29 young single mothers, many of whom were teenagers, were served with eviction notices from their specialist hostel in east London. The Focus E15 foyer provided one-bedroom apartments for the women to live in with their children, or whilst pregnant, after being made homeless, and provided targeted skills training, literacy teaching, and specialist support to help the women back into work or training. Many of the women in the £125-a-week rooms were studying, or in part-time work in the area, and one mother said she was applying for universities in London.

The funding of Supporting People, designed to help vulnerable people live independently, was slashed in England and the foyer said that without funding for specialist support, the hostel would cease to be an appropriate environment for young mothers and children. Newham Council, tasked with rehousing the women, told them they should expect to be placed outside the borough and city. A change to Newham's housing policy meant working families and people who had served in the armed forces received priority over single mothers like the Focus E15 residents.

Rather than accept their fate, the women took action. Starting from a weekly street stall in Stratford city centre, the women explained their predicament and soon rallied around supporters and other activists. This culminated in September 2014 with an attention-grabbing protest a few minutes' walk away next to Stratford station. Coinciding with London's Open House weekend, where iconic and listed buildings are opened to public tours, the Focus E15 campaigners, now comprising the mothers, locals, and seasoned campaigners, broke into two empty flats.

The flats, in the Carpenters Estate, had lain empty for years. Walking around the estate, it was remarkable how many windows were boarded up, so close to the 2012 Olympic site, which had promised regeneration and wealth for a poor area. Members of the Tenant Management Organisation, responsible for managing the site, told me Newham Council had refused to allow them to let properties that became empty if families moved out, slowly turning the red-brick estate into a ghost town.

Once in, the campaigners decorated the properties with toys, soft furnishings, banners and posters and declared their own Open House. Outside, green fabric banners decorated with the slogans "These Homes Need People: These People Need Homes" were unfurled, a simple message underlining the absurdity of the situation the mothers and other homeless families in the borough were faced with. On a sunny Saturday, the flats were thronged with visitors. One room I went into was being used as an impromptu crèche: babies were happily being entertained by two locals in a former bedroom. The living room was a campaign centre, with media phone numbers tacked to the wall, alongside lists of what was needed to make the occupation work.

What was striking about the flats was their state of repair. Curious visitors who popped in after hearing of the occupation via social media and news coverage were genuinely shocked at how immaculate the decor and fittings were. Wandering around, I noticed the wallpaper looked as good as new, and the kitchen was far better than many I had seen in my own rented flats over the years. The TMO said most flats were the same: perfectly liveable, but empty by command of the council. The campaigners pointed out that it would be far easier to move women into these small family homes than ship them miles from their own families, disrupting young children's lives.

The campaign garnered a huge amount of media and local attention, initially through social media, before being picked up by *The Guardian* and *The Financial Times*. In *The Guardian*, one of the mothers, Jasmin Stone, wrote:

> We wanted to participate in Open House to show how many houses sit empty in London and what an easy solution there is to the housing crisis. This crisis, as it is usually covered in the newspapers, is one experienced by the middle classes, whose

steady march from private renting to home ownership has been stopped in its tracks by the hugely inflated market. For members of the working class, however, the crisis is much more virulent. It involves not only the prospect of annual rent increases, the impossibility of home ownership and poor-quality housing, but also removal and displacement from the place in which you were born, leading to isolation in a place where you know nobody and opportunities for jobs are non-existent.[70]

The campaign, built up over years and still fighting homelessness and gentrification in Newham, meant that a process that usually happens to women silently was brought to public attention. Individually, families facing homelessness, often single mothers because they comprise the lowest-paid and most vulnerable households, are turned away from council housing offices and left to fend for themselves, or placed in unsuitable hostels miles away from their home. Focus E15 challenged this silencing and directly linked it to the rapid development of London due to unsustainably fast house-price growth tempting investors in to make a quick buck. Councils, with slashed budgets from central government, abdicate responsibility to vulnerable residents in lieu of making some quick cash from land sales, in the process (they hope) tempting in more financially flush tenants.

This exact scenario was relayed to me in 2010, when a Newham councillor asked me what I thought the biggest problem facing Newham was (I worked as a student welfare advisor in a university in the Borough). With students, predominantly women, coming in every day complaining about homelessness, poor conditions, or that they were experiencing domestic violence but couldn't afford to move out, I replied that the biggest issue was the need for more social housing. "Oh no", he said. "That just encourages undesirables." Instead, they needed to build more new, metropolitan flats, the kind springing up around Stratford Station and the under-development Westfield

Shopping Centre. The kind that attracted bankers from nearby Canary Wharf, not the sort of people who lived and worked in Newham already.

But "undesirables" have to live somewhere, and it sticks in the craw of the rich when these "undesirables" live in an area deemed desirable by the wealthy. The New Era estate in Hoxton was bought out in May 2014 by American property development company Westbrook Partners. Letters sent following the takeover informed the 93 families living on the estate that they faced a four-fold increase in rent. For the majority of the residents, this amounted to an eviction notice: few residents, some who had lived on the estate for as many as 70 years, could afford to pay those sums even if their only outgoing was rent.

Three women took charge of the fight to keep the residents in their homes: Lindsey Garrett, Danielle Molinari and Lynsay Spiteri rallied tenants and got word out about the conditions of the takeover. That the Benyon Estate, the family business of the country's richest MP, Richard Benyon, had a 10% stake in the estate made it easier to argue their case. The women contacted *The Daily Mirror*, then other papers, organised a demonstration outside Westbrook Partners' UK offices, and presented a 300,000-signature petition to Downing St.

After months of work, the campaign had won vocal and public support from politicians across the political divide, including the Mayor of London, Boris Johnson, and the Mayor of Hackney, the borough the estate resides in. For the investors, the level of attention and the volume of bad publicity made their plans untenable: shortly before Christmas, the Benyon Estate pulled out, quickly followed by Westbrook Partners. The estate was sold to Dolphin Square[71], a charity that is committed to providing low-cost homes to people on low incomes, and tenants were told not to expect rent increases.

Recovering from celebrations, Molinari told the BBC: "They underestimated us three women, but also all the residents on the estate, the community spirit and what Hoxton is all about".[72] Garrett, currently an NHS worker, is now planning to run for London Mayor in the 2016 elections, and has been elected chair of the New Era Tenants' Association.

The 3Cosas campaign have campaigned for better rights for cleaners (predominantly women) and fought gender discrimination and unfair dismissal cases when Unite the Union refused to recognise casual staff.

In 2013, the Home Office introduced a billboard van that drove around with the message "Here illegally? GO HOME" with a number listed for undocumented migrants to call. What the government termed the "Immigration Enforcement Campaign" quickly gained a new, more commonly used name: the "racist van". The glory of social media is that, as with the bedroom tax, you have little control over what people describe campaigns and policies as. Once the general public insists, by virtue of sheer wilful numbers, that they are going to use one term, your more strategic title is binned by most media outlets. One young woman, who writes pseudonymously as "Pukkah Punjabi", called the number, left a voicemail, then toyed with the Home Office operator who called her back, saying she was just after a lift back to Willesden, as that was her home. Social-media agitators continued to deluge the hotline with similar calls, until the campaign looked less Judge Dredd, more Benny Hill. Southall Black Sisters have campaigned for women for years and again hit the headlines on August 1st 2013, when they were holding a women's advice centre. Word reached the group of an immigration raid happening close by: the women gathered and drove the van away from their centre, before intercepting and surrounding the vans with supporters and megaphones as they attempted to carry out an immigration raid. "We were all so enraged by it that we emerged from our building and followed the vehicles around Southall shouting 'this is racist'," Southall Black Sisters wrote on their site. "Many of the women have escaped domestic violence and have felt trapped by their immigration status to stay in abusive marriages." Other groups have also worked to stop raids, notably the Anti-Raids Network, and often local communities act organically to attempt to stop raids, such as in south London in June 2015, when a UKBA van was surrounded, rocked, and had its tyres slashed by locals outraged at the attack on their community and neighbours.

These groups have secured victories and publicity, not by leaning in, behaving and striving individually, but by adopting very specific strategies. Direct action is key to each movement: while petitions and lobbying of local and national politicians have complemented each campaign, it is direct action that has put the cat amongst the pigeons, and allowed the women to fully expose the horror and unfairness of the causes they are highlighting and fighting for. If housing is your issue, why not occupy empty homes to show the claim there is nowhere for vulnerable women to go is a lie? If your community is being raided and your neighbours are being bundled into a van for deportation by state thugs, why let the UK Border Agency do so quietly? Show the world what is going on every day under their noses.

Social media has been a huge force in both mobilising and publicising campaigns and injustices. While a lot has been said about the abuse prominent women receive on the internet, the ability to get online and connect with potentially millions of people who would care about your cause if they heard about it is revolutionary. For women, the democratising potential of social media networks has helped bring attention to campaigns and causes that previously would have buckled without press attention. People speaking in real time, and consistently sharing information, has sustained and bolstered many campaigns. Politicians are still wary of social media: some have lost jobs over unwise outbursts, but there's also a fear of the unpredictable networks revealing actions (such as in Newham) that traditionally would have passed without outside notice or comment.

Mutual support and solidarity between neighbours and networks have been integral to many of these campaigns. Housing activists in different boroughs in London regularly disseminate email call-outs for more bodies and supplies for ongoing occupations around the capital. Actions against the UK Border Agency's immigration raids are only made possible by communities fighting back and refusing to see someone who lives or works alongside them dragged into a van only to disappear once deported. Again, social media allows bedroom-tax campaigners to discuss tactics and loopholes nationally and provide emotional support throughout fights to keep their home.

Media attention is still integral to a successful campaign, but has changed tack in recent years. Social media now drives much news — I've sat in many commissioning meetings where editors have been unenthused by a story, but journalists have pointed out it's all anyone is really discussing on social media, so choosing not to cover it looks politically motivated. A successful campaign thereby forces coverage, and coverage is the final stage in cementing victory. Politicians and forces will push not to recognise campaigns even when they're attracting mass attention, but the esteem for traditional media is still far higher, and often once newspapers or TV channels get involved, victory is not far away, as the New Era Estate campaign showed.

Sisters Uncut, Southall Black Sisters, and the bulk of housing and bedroom-tax campaigners are now women, and usually working-class women, often on benefits. They are at the vanguard of anti-austerity campaigning, refusing to accept the cuts that affect women disproportionately. While austerity may be temporary (though the Conservatives and Labour seem happy to accept that it is now ideologically permanent), the effect of austerity on women and children lasts a lifetime.

In her book on class and music culture in the Nineties, Rhian E Jones notes that class is an endemic problem in contemporary feminism:

> In mainstream politics and media, there remains a tendency for working-class women themselves to appear in feminist discourse as objects to be seen rather than heard, expected to rely on middle-class activists to articulate demands in their behalf but considered too inarticulate or otherwise "rough" to be directly engaged with.[73]

Will that change? Who knows. But the drive towards direct action by many groups run by women should be recognised as a constructive feminist movement, and will be by anyone sensible who recognises that gender is but one part of oppression.

By occupying, withdrawing labour, and refusing to be complicit in the state's violence against the most vulnerable in society, they show that "leaning out" of the capitalist model is far more effective at securing attention, provoking change, and ensuring demands are met than "leaning in". Few people ever get anything radical accomplished by continuing to play the game. The women on the frontline of the new feminist campaigning accept that capitalism and the political and power elites are no friend of women, and that to have a stab at a life that can support you and your children, the answer isn't to internalise the hatred society casts your way, but to fight to reveal injustice and refuse to participate.

CHAPTER 8

Conclusion

There's a tendency when you talk about women to assign them a homogenous identity, which never gets appended to men. Women are the softer sex, more caring, more body-conscious, more intuitive. Never mind that women are as complex in terms of identity as men. Much of the focus for feminism over the past decade or so has been either from the top down, or on the individual. The idea that women in power act for other women is not only insulting—men are rarely assumed to do so, and therefore are politicians rather than male politicians—but also neatly overlooks competing interests. A man in power is more likely to feel akin to another man in his position—a private-schooled, Oxbridge-educated professional—than a young, working-class, black fireman in Gateshead. Women in power generally come from the same set, and it's easier to assume your gender overrides the political ideology you align yourself with than admit that solidarity isn't automatic.

Criticism of any woman isn't anti-feminist purely because she is a woman: women occupy all sections of society now. The Queen being the Queen isn't an emancipatory feminist fact. Margaret Thatcher harmed more than helped women by becoming Prime Minister, drastically harming thousands of women's lives and communities because her class interests mattered far more to her than any modicum of gender solidarity. Sheryl Sandberg has worked for companies that are entrenching and worsening equality, but is able to cast herself as a feminist prophet because she has the money, power, and platform to do so, all the while refusing to engage with the structural and external forces perpetuating women's inequality, instead urging women to look inward. Why does this matter? Because feminism has become watered down, treated as a white-washing badge of honour rather than a radical emancipatory politics.

Feminism now means you don't always do the dishes, or that you look down your nose at women's magazines, rather than meaning you fight capitalist systems that enable continued attacks on the poorest and most vulnerable. It also enables you, in the same breath, to continue an imperialist worldview that condemns countries purely on the basis of how they treat women, without stopping to consider whether the corporations you laud for hiring women in one country are causing mass hardship for women in sweatshops in another.

Media narratives around feminism would do well to consider whether political messages on poverty and welfare do far more harm than the much derided women's magazines and lads' mags that are attacked increasingly by some feminists. The attacks on women's magazines seem to assume a gullibility amongst their female readers that is insulting and sexist within itself, believing that all messages and articles are read with po-faced sincerity and accepted wholesale. Women are savvy readers, and don't need protection from satire or fluff. Similarly, a focus on "sexualisation" and objectification often falls back to the argument that thin models are fuelling eating disorders, when the evidence shows eating disorders are far more about self-control and psychological trauma than a diet gone wrong.

The constant drip-feed of stories about women on benefits living in now-expensive areas, or women with multiple children and out of work, further demonises the poor, who are disproportionately women. Once demonised, people end up disenfranchised: if society is keen to tell you they think you are human waste, you internalise that message and stop fighting back.

But actually, many people — and especially women — are fighting back. Rather than leaning in and trying to forge a path within structures that are so hostile to them, they're leaning out and refusing to play the game anymore. Women out of work are organising to fight cuts in their areas; homeless women are fighting back and refusing to accept being shunted off to a city miles from home like so much unwanted flotsam; women are forming networks that recognise capitalism is the problem, not the answer, and that the way to fight for women's rights is to become a thorn in the side, instead of the grease in a cog.

Ultimately, all Sheryl Sandberg's vision of leaning in offers is an OK job, and the opportunity to see your children at the same time. In terms of ambition, it's sorely lacking. Both aims are meagre and quite frankly dull, if that's all a dream amounts to. Fighting for equality is often misunderstood as simply being offered the same terms as men on paper. In many ways we already have that. What we don't have is emancipation: the opportunity to be free of social and external shackles that perpetuate inequality and women's lower position. Women around the world now are demanding more: paid work, a life for their children, but also the right to be listened to, a political voice, direct democracy, and the right to a full civic life. That isn't won by keeping quiet: it's won by physically and psychologically going on strike, by shouting back, and leaning out.

ACKNOWLEDGMENTS

Far too many friends offered advice and encouragement while writing, especially Jennifer Tighe, Daniel Trilling, James Butler, Alice Spawls, Andrea Solomon, Juliet Jacques, Eben Marks, Jo Biggs, Tupon Bhowmik, Suzanne Moore, Paul Myerscough, Harry Stopes, Danny Dorling, and Sarah Shin.

Special thanks are reserved for my colleagues and editors at Repeater: Tamar Shlaim, Alex Niven, and Tariq Goddard. And at *The Guardian* to Becky Gardiner who is as sharply intelligent as she is charming, and Natalie Hanman, whose faith and commissioning nous first gave me the idea for the book, but most of all to Alison Benjamin, who is entirely to blame for the fact that I am a journalist and writer.

REFERENCES

1 https://www.dissentmagazine.org/online_articles/feminisms-tipping-point-who-wins-from-leaning-in

2 https://www.washingtonpost.com/opinions/sheryl-sandbergs-lean-in-campaign-holds-little-for-most-women/2013/02/25/c584c9d2-7f51-11e2-a350-49866afab584_story.html

3 http://www.theguardian.com/commentisfree/2014/feb/13/lean-in-character-education-poverty

4 https://www.jacobinmag.com/2013/03/like-feminism/

5 http://www.strategyand.pwc.com/global/home/what-we-think/reports-white-papers/article-display/2013-chief-executive-study

6 http://www.theguardian.com/business/2011/sep/08/carol-bartz-blast-yahoo-after-being-fired

7 https://opendemocracy.net/5050/emily-thomson-and-susanne-ross/women-postrecession-moving-towards-insecurity

8 http://www.newrepublic.com/article/112610/sheryl-sandberg-and-lean-folly-davos-feminism

9 Nicole Ascherhoff, *New Prophets of Capital*, Verso Books 2015.

10 htttp://www.ft.com/cms/s/0/be7a0b6e-16f2-11e3-9ec2-00144feabdc0.html

11 http://www.theguardian.com/politics/2013/oct/12/labour-benefits-tories-labour-rachel-reeves-welfare

12 http://www.theatlantic.com/magazine/archive/2012/07/why-women-still-cant-have-it-all/309020/

13 http://www.theguardian.com/society/2013/sep/21/spending-cuts-women-report

14 http://www.theguardian.com/business/2013/nov/01/young-women-trapped-low-paid-skilled-jobs

15 http://www.theguardian.com/money/2013/jun/12/workers-deepest-cuts-real-wages-ifs

16 https://www.gov.uk/government/uploads/system/uploads/attachment_data/file/31480/11-745-women-on-boards.pdf

17 http://www.theguardian.com/business/2013/dec/11/women-missing-out-on-senior-boardroom-roles

18 http://www.theguardian.com/business/2011/jul/01/norway-golden-skirt-quota-boardroom

19 http://highpaycentre.org/files/REVISED_WOMEN_ON_BOARDS.pdf

20 Nancy Fraser, *Fortunes of Feminism*. Verso Books, 2013.

21 Sheryl Sandberg, *Lean In*. WH Allen, 2013. p. 128

22 ibid p. 102

23 http://www.theguardian.com/news/datablog/2013/oct/25/world-gender-gap-index-2013-countries-compare-iceland-uk

24 http://sweden.se/society/gender-equality-in-sweden/

25 http://www.ft.com/cms/s/0/be7a0b6e-16f2-11e3-9ec2-00144feabdc0.html#axzz2lHtjPXz9

26 http://www.qmul.ac.uk/media/news/items/hss/79302.html

27 http://www.includegender.org/

28 http://www.nytimes.com/2013/06/05/world/europe/progress-for-women-in-norway-but-a-long-way-to-go.html?_r=0

29 http://www.amnesty.org/en/library/info/ACT77/001/2010

30 http://www.thelocal.se/20131104/foster-home-rape-case-acquittal-courts-controversy

31 http://www.thelocal.se/20130930/50526

32 http://jezebel.com/attention-women-and-minorities-leave-diverse-hiring-to-1609649160

33 https://www.jacobinmag.com/2014/06/pink-collar/

34 https://www.jacobinmag.com/2014/06/pink-collar/

35 http://www.adweek.com/prnewser/in-pr-women-outnumber-men-but-men-still-earn-more/6707

36 Joanna Biggs, *All Day Long: A Portrait of Britain at Work*. Profile Books, 2015.

37 https://www.citizensadvice.org.uk/about-us/how-citizens-advice-works/media/press-releases/employment-tribunal-costs-putting-people-off-valid-claims/

38 Danny Dorling, *Inequality and the 1%*. Verso Books, 2014.

39 http://www.theguardian.com/commentisfree/2015/jul/12/gavin-kelly-raising-pay-slashing-benefits-working-poor

40 http://www.channel4.com/news/yarls-wood-immigration-removal-detention-centre-investigation

41 http://www.bbc.co.uk/news/uk-33043395

42 http://www.theguardian.com/uk-news/2015/apr/25/yarls-wood-guard-suspended-over-alleged-assault-on-women

43 http://www.theguardian.com/uk-news/2015/mar/03/yarls-wood-may-state-sanctioned-abuse-women

44 http://www.theguardian.com/commentisfree/2008/oct/28/equality-gender

45 https://www.opendemocracy.net/5050/barbara-gunnell/how-women-are-paying-for-recession-in-uk

46 http://www.bbc.co.uk/news/uk-25195914

47 http://www.womensaid.org.uk/page.
asp?section=0001000100100022&sectiontitle=sos

48 http://www.independent.co.uk/news/thatchers-dad-mayor-
preacher-groper-1257249.html

49 http://www.theguardian.com/uk-news/2015/feb/26/jimmy-savile-
given-free-rein-to-sexually-abuse-60-people-report-finds

50 http://www.bbc.co.uk/news/uk-politics-23355531

51 http://www.newyorker.com/business/currency/lean-ins-business-
friendly-message

52 http://www.theguardian.com/commentisfree/2015/apr/09/sorry-
dove-personal-care-product-choose-beautiful-campaign

53 http://www.nytimes.com/2011/11/23/opinion/pinkwashing-and-
israels-use-of-gays-as-a-messaging-tool.html?_r=0

54 http://www.theguardian.com/world/2002/sep/21/gender.usa

55 http://www.theguardian.com/world/feminism

56 Nina Power, *One Dimensional Woman*. Zero Books, 2009.

57 Linda R Hirschman, *Get To Work*. Viking, 2006. p. 1–2.

58 http://www.theguardian.com/books/2011/jun/24/feminism-21st-
century-zoe-williams

59 http://www.theguardian.com/commentisfree/2012/oct/11/david-
cameron-aspiration-nation

60 http://www.ippr.org/press-releases/111/10581/twentieth-century-
feminism-failed-working-class-women

61 http://www.theguardian.com/society/2013/mar/31/gender-pay-
feminism-working-class?guni=article:in%2520body%2520olink

62 http://www.opendemocracy.net/5050/heather-mcrobie/when-
austerity-sounds-like-backlash-gender-and-economic-crisis

63 http://www.theguardian.com/society/2013/sep/21/spending-cuts-
women-report

64 http://www.theguardian.com/money/2013/jun/12/workers-
deepest-cuts-real-wages-ifs

65 http://www.theguardian.com/commentisfree/2013/dec/09/black-
feminist-movement-fails-women-black-minority

66 http://www.theguardian.com/lifeandstyle/2013/nov/16/feminism-
rebranding-lucy-mangan

67 http://rhianejones.com/2013/11/26/things-that-shouldnt-need-
saying-slight-return/

68 http://www.fawcettsociety.org.uk/wp-content/uploads/2013/02/
The-Impact-of-Austerity-on-Women-19th-March-2012.pdf

69 http://www.theguardian.com/society/2014/oct/20/britain-future-divided-rich-poor-poverty-commission-report
70 http://www.theguardian.com/commentisfree/2014/sep/23/why-occupying-boarded-up-east-london-council-house-social-housing
71 http://www.theguardian.com/society/2014/dec/19/new-era-residents-celebrate-charity-buys-estate-investor
72 http://www.bbc.co.uk/news/uk-30563265
73 Rhian E Jones, *Clampdown: Pop-Cultural Wars on Class and Gender*. Zero Books, 2013.

Repeater Books

is dedicated to the creation of a new reality. The landscape of twenty-first-century arts and letters is faded and inert, riven by fashionable cynicism, egotistical self-reference and a nostalgia for the recent past. Repeater intends to add its voice to those movements that wish to enter history and assert control over its currents, gathering together scattered and isolated voices with those who have already called for an escape from Capitalist Realism. Our desire is to publish in every sphere and genre, combining vigorous dissent and a pragmatic willingness to succeed where messianic abstraction and quiescent co-option have stalled: abstention is not an option: we are alive and we don't agree.